GHOST TOWNS OF THE NORTHWEST
Known and Unknown

OTHER BOOKS BY THE AUTHOR:
All About Grizzly Bears
All About The White-Tailed Deer
Helldorados, Ghosts and Camps of the Old Southwest

Ghost Towns *of the* Northwest

By

NORMAN D. WEIS

PHOTOGRAPHS AND MAPS BY THE AUTHOR

The CAXTON PRINTERS, Ltd.
CALDWELL, IDAHO
1977

First printing May, 1971
Second printing April, 1972
Third printing June, 1974
Fourth printing May, 1977

International Standard Book Number 0-87004-201-7

Library of Congress Catalog Card No. 75-137768

Lithographed and bound in the United States of America by
The CAXTON PRINTERS, Ltd.
Caldwell, Idaho   83605
130462

To J. M. W.

PREFACE

GHOST TOWNS are quiet places. Little or nothing moves about. This characteristic is faithfully preserved—in fact enhanced—through the process of still photography. Mediocre scenes of deserted buildings seem to gain quality through the developing process. Imposing remains, backed by puffy clouds, become near classics. It is the stillness of ghost towns that appeals to the maker of pictures.

This book is a collection of photographs, with a little history, adventure and humor sandwiched randomly between. The historical accounts included are as accurate as the reference sources available, and as reliable as the individuals interviewed. In the belief that history need not be tedious or boring, I have attempted to slip the facts in painlessly—in some cases almost subliminally. The humor fell in place quite by accident. Old-timers remembered first the tall tales, then the fact, and often the facts were hilarious. Prone to stupid mistakes, and suffering from a mild case of "foot in mouth disease," I contributed my own share of misunderstandings and embarrassing moments.

A writer may quite accidentally mislead his readers by extolling the past glories of a particular ghost town while excluding any mention of its present remains. Numerous old photos complete the illusion, and the reader is convinced that the town is worth at least a weekend visit. Too often I have traveled more than one hundred miles to explore such well-described sites, only to find that a dam built forty years ago put it under eighty feet of water, or that a bowling alley had been built on its bulldozed remains, and it in turn had been burned to the ground. For this reason the photographs in this book are accurate renditions of present remains. A few old photos have been included, but they are clearly labeled as such.

Between ten and fifteen ghost towns from each of the five Northwest States were chosen to be treated in this book. Some well-known favorites were included. At these sites, the effort was primarily on a new approach to a well-known story, or an elaboration on some new aspect freshly uncovered.

A concerted effort was made to search out some "unknowns" in each state—towns that have had little or no mention in print. A large part of the text is devoted to the search for these sites and their subsequent exploration. That is where the adventure comes in.

The effort, of course, was not all mine, and I am privileged to thank those whose assistance was so willingly given. Suggestions concerning the text, solicited of Mike Herbison and Marie Stewart, were of great help. Wilhelm Ossa and Joe Stewart gave valuable advice on the selection of photographs. Senator Gale McGee, of Wyoming, was instrumental in procuring the topographic maps vital to the search for "unknown" sites. There were many who offered help and hospitality along the way, and to them I have expressed my appreciation in the text. Here are some folk, not otherwise mentioned, who deserve my thanks:

Mr. Antonioli, of Butte, Montana, owner of Kirkville, Montana.

The unnamed old-timer at Galena, Idaho, who shared with me a very welcome pot of coffee on a rainy afternoon.

Gale Ontko of the Bureau of Land Management, Prineville, Oregon.

Mr. and Mrs. Paul Corbaley, of Blewett, Washington.

John Meek, of Boulder, Colorado.

Mr. and Mrs. Moerer, of Atlantic City, Wyoming.

The personnel of the State Archives, Museums, and Libraries of Oregon, Washington, Idaho, Wyoming, and Montana.

The U.S. Weather Bureau employees, of Bozeman, Montana, who gave me access to satellite photos and helped me determine how to escape the cloud-hiding smoke of forest fires drifting down from Canada and Alaska.

Numerous mine engineers, hoist operators, muckers, and prospectors, especially the old hand I met in northern Idaho who proudly showed me his three peanut-butter jars full of gold nuggets.

Lastly, for adding a little spice to life, I would like to thank the two eighty-year-old citizens of a once booming town in southern Wyoming, who, insulted at my suggestion that their town was nearly a ghost, stood up as one and challenged me to a fight!

CONTENTS

ILLUSTRATIONS

INTRODUCTION

FOR SEVERAL YEARS the exact definition of the term "ghost town" has eluded me. A ghost town should, of course, display only a shadow of its former glory. Ideally it would be completely deserted, full of two- and three-story false-fronted buildings, all of them completely furnished and undisturbed. The town should appear as if the entire population had gone to a funeral and failed to return. To top it off, a tumbleweed should blow down the dusty main street, bouncing in rhythm with the banging of loose shutters and the screech of unoiled hinges.

But that's not the way it is. Perhaps such a perfect example awaits discovery, but I fear that I shall never find it. I've seen the tumbleweed, but the buildings were mere heaps of rubble. The rattling shutters were there, too, but the buildings were single-storied and empty of wares. Three-story false-fronted buildings? Yes, but the town was yet alive.

About the closest I could come to a proper definition was that "the place excited me." Excited me enough to recommend that others travel perhaps fifty miles to see it. It is a poor definition, and I'm happy to swap it for one proposed quite offhand by a gentleman from Spray, Oregon.

I called him "The Sage from Spray" because he had a constructive, although caustic comment to make on every subject broached. He watched as I spread maps out on the counter. He listened as I asked questions about some of the towns in the vicinity. A number of interested folk volunteered information on this and that town, designating several as genuine ghost towns. Finally the "Sage" took issue. "Hell, I don't see how you guys can call them places ghost towns! They's just like any other town 'cept they ain't hardly no one livin' there. . . ."

Part of the fascination of ghost-town hunting comes from the wide array of hazards involved. Bad roads are the rule, and a four-wheel-drive vehicle is a must. But four-wheel-drive is of little comfort when ruts are deep enough to let the differentials drag. With the slightest effort, one can become high-centered, spinning all four wheels free and clear. On back roads, distances between gas stations can be unbelievable. When the tank gauge reads "zero," one becomes apprehensive, but the addition of a five-gallon reserve tank of gas wipes out all fears. But soon the gauge reads "zero" again, and your goal changes from deserted towns to "some sign of civilization." Miraculously, I never had to walk for gas. Often the tank read less than empty when a service station was finally reached. Each time I marked the needle's position with a felt pen. At the end of two months, I had a fan-shaped array of marks extending to what should have been a minus one-quarter tank.

Having taken precautions concerning oil (four extra quarts) and gas, the only mechanical trouble was dislocation of the drive-shaft support. Located in the exact center of the vehicle, it was vulnerable to any rock more than six inches high. Ten or twelve hard whacks with a one-pound sledge always put it back in reasonable position. After half a dozen straightenings, it began to weaken, and finally had to be replaced.

Some problems encountered while ghost-town hunting are compounded by the bad habits common to most photographers. Often looking through the viewfinder, and seldom watching their feet, they are forever backing up while looking forward. Snakes and open shafts abound—and nails—nails are there by the thousand, firmly embedded and pointing straight up, each one a rusty invitation to lockjaw.

By far the greatest obstacle facing the would-be visitor to a ghost town is initially locating the site. A search of the existing literature will reveal the obvious towns, and an in-depth investigation into the records and photos in various state archives will turn up a few more, also quite well known. Post office records and county seat plat books will give up their share of secrets. Fishermen, hunters, bottle diggers, state patrolmen, and of course the old-timers are valuable sources for searching out the lesser known sites. Old-timers are often difficult to locate, but it is worth the effort, for the benefits are twofold. As one proceeds to gather information on sites already visited, clues to additional ghost towns come to light.

None of the aforementioned methods is quite as produc-

tive as a systematic search of topographic maps. Multitudes
of "possibles" can be pinpointed for later investigation. The
United States Geological Survey (U.S.G.S.) maps are among
the most responsive to careful analysis. A complete set of
such maps for a given state are available at most libraries.
The job of searching each map—square mile by square mile
—can be tedious. A map may require a mere ten minutes
of study, but there are many maps to scan. There are more
than 850 U.S.G.S. maps for the state of Montana alone.

The most common is the 7½ minute map, labeled because it encompasses 7½ minutes of longitude and latitude.
These terms are not important as long as one realizes that
such a map covers an area approximately six miles east and
west, by nine miles north and south. The scale is listed as
1:24,000, but is more easily understood as approximately
2½ inches to the mile. That is quite a large and revealing
scale. Every building is shown as a square, filled in if occupied, and empty if empty. Forests are shown in green
overlay. Surveyors claim that even a three-foot bush is rep-
resented by a tiny green dot. Contour lines indicate the
steepness of slope. Where they lie close, the grade is steep
—where there are few, it is relatively level. Every creek,
ridge, road, railroad, shaft, tunnel, and prospect hole is sup-
posed to be indicated, but map-makers do make mistakes.
Buildings are left out and extra lakes are occasionally
thrown in. Once a feature is listed on a map, it is generally
carried along through future revisions. This perpetuation
makes most maps accidentally historical in nature. The
original map date is always listed, and one may assume any
buildings shown were actually in existence on that date.
When a topo map shows a town of considerable outlay, and
the same town is missing or indicated minimally on a road
map, then it may be considered a possible ghost town worthy of investigation. Other signs that tip off the presence
of a ghost town are dead-end roads and railroads, mine
shafts, tunnels, and prospect holes. Unnamed buildings
set in a row often indicate a company town. Tailings denoted
by small "v" shaped marks are sure indications of a past
mining effort. The very name of a town is indicative. You
may ignore "Kennedy Heights" and "Plaza Park," as they
are sure to be modern communities, but "Galena," "Iron-
ton," and "Copperopolis" are good bets. It has been my
experience that if chosen carefully, about 25 percent of the
sites selected prove to be ghost towns. The percentage is

enhanced by the cartographer's occasional use of the terms "abandoned" or "site."

The U.S.G.S. publishes many maps of lesser scale that cover larger territories. The 15 minute map covers an area approximately thirteen by eighteen miles and its scale is approximately one inch to the mile. Harder to read than the 7½ minute map, it is still valuable, and is often the only topo map available.

The two maps reproduced here are typical examples of the 7½ and 15 minute topos. Each map has the important items labeled and explained. If you can remember that the top of a map is north, and that each red square is a square mile, the rest is easy.

Topographic maps may be obtained through local retailers, but stocks are often limited. The Denver section of the U.S.G.S. offers for sale all the maps covering the Western United States. The address:

> Denver Distribution Section
> U.S. Geological Survey
> Denver Federal Center—Building 41
> Denver, Colorado   80225

Upon request, free copies of state index maps will be supplied. Desired maps can be readily selected with the aid of these "keys." The prices of topo maps are generally fifty cents each, with discounts on quantity orders.

This is a portion of the *Radium Springs, Wyoming 7½ minute* topographic map. Dirt roads are shown as solid double lines. The dashed lines indicate unimproved dirt roads or trails. Item A proved to be "The Good Hope Mine," a most scenic relic. B indicates The Oregon Trail. Note the Trail merging with the road, then passing through Lewiston, item D. Little is known of this remote Wyoming ghost town, and small bits of information gleaned from maps are often important. There were two very old log buildings just as indicated, one a false-fronted store, the other a livery. E is "The Hidden Hand Mine," conveniently labeled and complete with hoist house and smithy. F indicates another mine not shown on the map. Named "The Iron Duke," it would be a nameless site except for persevering memories of old-timers living in the area. Items H and I represent a small mining complex and extensive tailings. One of the buildings by the mine shaft is the home of the only surviving prospector on the Sweetwater River. Items C and G proved to be insignificant.

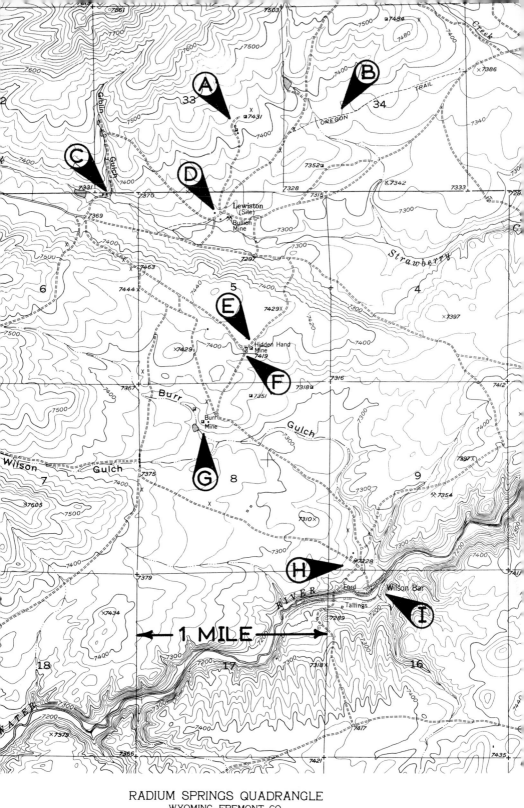

RADIUM SPRINGS QUADRANGLE
WYOMING–FREMONT CO.
7.5 MINUTE SERIES (TOPOGRAPHIC)

Approximately one-fourth of the *Bodie Mountain, Washington, 15 minute* topographic map is shown here.

Upon investigation, Item A turned out to be a mixture of old sawmill remains and relatively modern cabins. It was clearly not a ghost town. B, labeled "Bodie," is a small but well-known ghost town. The building on the left is a schoolhouse. Those on the right are old stores and residences of Bodie, some of which have been converted to vacation homes. C is "Old Toroda." Only one building is shown on the map. Actually there are a number of buildings at the site, making Old Toroda a ghost town worth visiting. The "Old Sheridan Mine," D, was indeed old, and consisted of far more than was shown on the map. Item F is the town of Sheridan, one of the finest "unknown" ghost towns visited. The two empty buildings indicated on the map are large 2½ story log structures. In addition, there are nearly a dozen other buildings standing in town, along with a fancy frame hotel, now partially collapsed. Item E was not visited, due to over-indulgence concerning Item F.

Finding the site on the map is the first step—getting there is often a difficult second. New roads frequently make access to old roads difficult. Eroded trails and locked gates can stop the best of backcountry vehicles, but there is little to inhibit foot travel. Walking is time-consuming and tiring, and the trail seems always to be steep. A five-mile hike may be required to reach a deserted site, and, often as not, one will find the old town has been newly converted to a ski resort, accessed from the other side of the hill by an excellent blacktop road.

Once found, photographing the site is a simple matter. Film is cheap compared to gasoline, so plenty of variations in angle and exposure are in order. Clouds add tremendously to most scenes, but like a watched pot, clouds are slow to cooperate when closely observed. A paperback book was an item of standard equipment. A dozen pages always seemed to lure the clouds into proper position. Plus X pan professional film was preferred for the black and white photographs, and was exposed through a yellow 2 X filter. Ektachrome X was used for the color shots. The Praktisix 2¼x2¼ reflex camera was my favorite. It handled well and produced pictures equal in quality to that of cameras costing three times as much. Absolutely necessary are a penta-prism for eye-level composition, and a monopod or tripod for a steady hold through the exposure. The monopod is

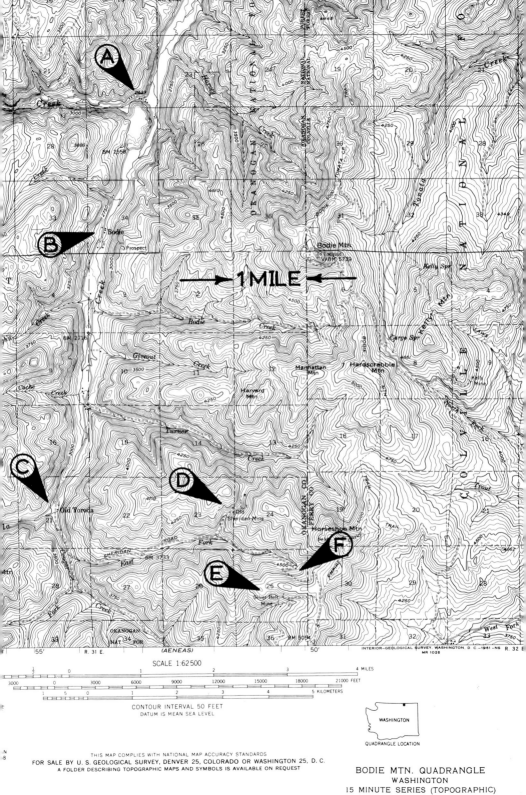

SCALE 1:62500

CONTOUR INTERVAL 50 FEET
DATUM IS MEAN SEA LEVEL

THIS MAP COMPLIES WITH NATIONAL MAP ACCURACY STANDARDS
FOR SALE BY U. S. GEOLOGICAL SURVEY, DENVER 25, COLORADO OR WASHINGTON 25, D. C.
A FOLDER DESCRIBING TOPOGRAPHIC MAPS AND SYMBOLS IS AVAILABLE ON REQUEST

WASHINGTON

QUADRANGLE LOCATION

BODIE MTN. QUADRANGLE
WASHINGTON
15 MINUTE SERIES (TOPOGRAPHIC)

TOPOGRAPHIC MAP SYMBOLS

VARIATIONS WILL BE FOUND ON OLDER MAPS

Hard surface, heavy duty road, four or more lanes . . . . . .

Hard surface, heavy duty road, two or three lanes . . . .

Hard surface, medium duty road, four or more lanes . . . .

Hard surface, medium duty road, two or three lanes . . . . .

Improved light duty road . . . .

Unimproved dirt road and trail . . . .

Dual highway, dividing strip 25 feet or less . . . .

Dual highway, dividing strip exceeding 25 feet . . . .

Road under construction . . . .

Railroad, single track and multiple track . . . .

Railroads in juxtaposition . . . .

Narrow gage, single track and multiple track . . . .

Railroad in street and carline . . . .

Bridge, road and railroad . . . .

Drawbridge, road and railroad . . . .

Footbridge . . . .

Tunnel, road and railroad . . . .

Overpass and underpass . . . .

Important small masonry or earth dam . . . .

Dam with lock . . . .

Dam with road . . . .

Canal with lock . . . .

Buildings (dwelling, place of employment, etc.) . . . .

School, church, and cemetery . . . . Cem

Buildings (barn, warehouse, etc.) . . . .

Power transmission line . . . .

Telephone line, pipeline, etc. (labeled as to type) . . . .

Wells other than water (labeled as to type) . . . . oOil . . . . . oGas

Tanks; oil, water, etc. (labeled as to type) . . . . • • ● ⊘Water

Located or landmark object; windmill . . . . o

Open pit, mine, or quarry; prospect . . . . ✕ x

Shaft and tunnel entrance . . . . ▪ . . . . . . Y

Horizontal and vertical control station:

Tablet, spirit level elevation . . . . BM △ 5653

Other recoverable mark, spirit level elevation . . . . △ 5455

Horizontal control station: tablet, vertical angle elevation VABM △ 9519

Any recoverable mark, vertical angle or checked elevation △ 3775

Vertical control station: tablet, spirit level elevation . . . . . BM ✕ 957

Other recoverable mark, spirit level elevation . . . . ✕ 954

Checked spot elevation . . . . ✕ 4675

Unchecked spot elevation and water elevation . . . . ✕ 5657 . . . . 8'0

Boundary, national . . . .

State . . . .

County, parish, municipio . . . .

Civil township, precinct, town, barrio . . . .

Incorporated city, village, town, hamlet . . . .

Reservation, national or state . . . .

Small park, cemetery, airport, etc. . . . .

Land grant . . . .

Township or range line, United States land survey . . . . .

Township or range line, approximate location . . . .

Section line, United States land survey . . . .

Section line, approximate location . . . .

Township line, not United States land survey . . . .

Section line, not United States land survey . . . .

Section corner, found and indicated . . . . +

Boundary monument: land grant and other . . . . ▫

United States mineral or location monument . . . .

Index contour . . . . Intermediate contour . .

Supplementary contour Depression contours . .

Fill . . . . Cut . . . .

Levee . . . . Levee with road . . . . .

Mine dump . . . . Wash . . . .

Tailings . . . . Tailings pond . . . .

Strip mine . . . . Distorted surface . . . .

Sand area . . . . Gravel beach . . . .

Perennial streams . . . . . Intermittent streams . .

Elevated aqueduct . . . . . Aqueduct tunnel . . . . .

Water well and spring . o . . . . o Disappearing stream . .

Small rapids . . . . Small falls . . . .

Large rapids . . . . Large falls . . . .

Intermittent lake . . . . . Dry lake . . . .

Foreshore flat . . . . Rock or coral reef . . . .

Sounding, depth curve . . 10 Piling or dolphin . . . . .

Exposed wreck . . . . Sunken wreck . . . .

Rock, bare or awash; dangerous to navigation . . . . *

Marsh (swamp) . . . . Submerged marsh . . . . .

Wooded marsh . . . . Mangrove . . . .

Woods or brushwood . . Orchard . . . .

Vineyard . . . . Scrub . . . .

Inundation area . . . . Urban area . . . .

the more mobile of the two devices, and the single leg is steady enough, when the camera is braced against the forehead, to allow exposures as slow as one-thirtieth of a second. A roll of 120 film takes twelve shots, and the average ghost town required four rolls. To keep the records straight, it was my practice to write the name of the town on the outside of each roll of exposed film. Later I realized that the outer portion was discarded during development, and the record lost. The solution was simple—write the name of the town on some convenient surface, then photograph the sign. Each new roll was started with one exposure sacrificed in the interest of accurate records. I have chalked names of ghost towns on boards, old buckets, barrels, and outhouse walls. In a pinch, I have used the black sidewalls of my truck tires. Although of short duration, and certain to wash away, the chalked names might have appeared to be the work of some demented soul bent on visiting and repeatedly identifying every deserted town in the Northwest.

Perhaps that statement is not too far off the mark. Although this book is not intended to be comprehensive, more than two hundred sites were visited. I selected three or four dozen from each of the five states, taking care to choose among them ten well-known sites. The remainder were "possible unknowns" gleaned from searching the topographic maps. Of these "possibles," a number turned out to be lively communities. Many others had been completely eradicated by civilization. About one in four was a genuine ghost town. Of the sites visited, I selected sixty-two for inclusion in this book. They were chosen for their story, their photogenic qualities, or for their virginity of publication.

Four times these ghost towns have come to life for me— when found and studied during the map search, when visited and researched, when photographs came to life in the darkroom, and finally when the text was assembled from notes and reference.

My sincere hope is that your enjoyment one time through will equal the four of mine.

PART I
OREGON

OREGON AREA 1

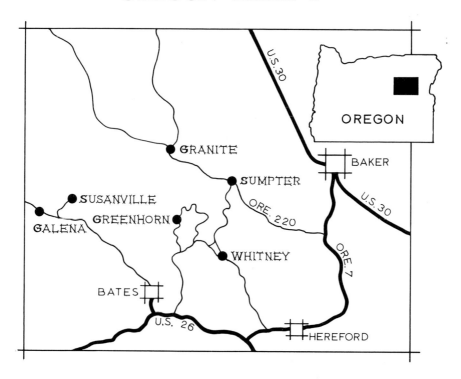

SUMPTER, OREGON

AT SHORT GLANCE, the old dredge resembled a monster. A
monster in its last frantic moment of life, its square-browed
head reared high, vacant eyes staring blindly, with steel
jaws poised for a last vengeful thrust.

Frozen in position by disuse, and trapped in a small pond
of its own making, the gigantic dredge is as impressive as
the destruction still evident in its gravel-strewn wake. This
dredge, and two others like it, once ravaged the broad valley of the Powder River of eastern Oregon. Green with
tree and lush with grass, the terrain was lifted, sifted,
washed, and subtracted of its wealth, then haphazardly replaced. The precious soil that once topped the baser rock
now spreads its fertility thinly downstream. Gold was the
master, and ten tons of it lay in the valley, demanding harvest. The giant dredges reaped that harvest, slowly tracing
their broad erosionary swaths until the entire valley was
consumed.

The last survivor of a trio of dredges that sifted the gravels
of Powder River below Sumpter. Note the remains
of the old gangplank in center foreground.

*The bridge, or control house, sits atop the machinery decks and affords
a necessary view of the endless chain of steel buckets that fed a
continuing shower of gold-bearing gravel into the dredge's maw.*

Twelve million dollars' worth of gold poured temporary
life into the town of Sumpter. That life has since faded, and
little is left of the original Sumpter. One of the three
dredges was destroyed by fire, another dismantled and
shipped to richer gravel. The third dredge is intact,
and is Sumpter's largest and most impressive surviving
structure. It rests quietly in the small pond at the east edge
of town. Slightly down at the bow and in gentle contact
with the bottom, its endless bucket chain is raised high.
Three levels of enclosed machinery topped with a control
house, which in turn is capped by a cable housing, give the
dredge a height fully sixty feet above waterline.

As I was preparing to photograph the old relic, a man and
two boys approached. Equipped with hammers, gold pans,
and fishing tackle, they proceeded to unlock the sliding door
on the lower deck. As part owners of the dredge, they were
intent on enjoying the day aboard their private, although

*The hospital was one of the few buildings to escape the fire
of 1916. It was later converted to an I.O.O.F. Hall.*

immobile craft. I quickly accepted their invitation to tour the monster's innards.

An ancient electric motor once fed power to the chain of buckets by means of a drive belt eighty feet long, two feet wide, and nearly a half an inch thick. Great banks of shakers and sorters processed the gravel to a gold-bearing black sand concentrate. Next, scavenger jigs separated the gold from the useless sand. One of the cogwheels that relayed power to the shakers was thirteen feet in diameter. From the broad-windowed bridge, the operator controlled all functions with twelve large levers and a number of rheostats. A double-barreled heater constructed from two fifty-gallon drums offered minimal comfort on cold days. A catwalk led directly from the control deck to the extreme end of the dredge boom. A serpentine stairway connected the bridge with the lower machine decks. The handrails were worn pleasantly smooth from countless use.

A small projection at water level, "amidships on the port side," made an ideal fishing platform for one of the boys. Although small, the trout were plentiful. The boy's brother and father were busy pounding out rust and trace deposits left in the final shakers and scavenger jigs. It took an hour or so for them to glean a cup of rusty concentrate, but when panned, the gold realized was enough to pay wages, and to set them once again to pounding away at the old rusted machinery.

Gold was located here in 1862 by a group of Confederate soldiers on their way to California. They called the place Sumter, after the fort of the same name. Later the spelling was changed to the present Sumpter. News of their discovery of placer gold spread rapidly, and soon hundreds of men were washing gravel. In the late seventies the Chinese moved in to rework the same deposits. Later, the prime deposits were found on the hillsides, and hard-rock mining ensued. In 1896 the railroad reached town, and the population grew to more than three thousand. Sumpter town reached its maximum in 1900 when the deep mines and the dredges were both operating full shifts.

There were two brick banks, two hotels, an opera house, a lumber mill, and more than two dozen saloons in Sumpter. A two-story building on the hill served as a hospital, and was later converted to an Odd Fellows Hall.

The fire of 1916 destroyed most of Sumpter. When the hoses burned through, dynamite was used to blow up build-

A study in contrasts. The barn, probably more than a century old, is topped by a modern air marker pointing the way to the nearest airport twenty-one miles away.

The brick building now used as a town hall was once a store with office space above. The small structure in front is the Sumpter Fire Department, complete with "modernized hose cart."

ings to create firebreaks. The desperate attempt to save the
town largely failed, and only a few structures were saved.
The Odd Fellows Hall, the school, a store, a few barns, and a
number of residences were among the survivors. Many
citizens moved out. Those who stayed scavenged many of
the deserted buildings to enhance their own homes, or to
supply firewood for the winter.

One of the surviving barns has been preserved by the care
demanded by constant use, and the protection of a metal
roof. Painted on the roof, in startling contrast, is an orange-
lettered sign marking the location and distance to the nearest airport. It seems as incongruous as an old man wearing
a propellor beanie. Alongside is parked an old, solid-rubber-
tired Union Oil trailer tank.

An old brick vault marks the location of one of the town's
banks. Nearby is a small wooden shed with a bashed-in
garage door at its front. This is Sumpter's fire department.
Inside is a brightly painted four-wheeled trailer with a
tongue adapted to either pulling by hand or attaching by pin
and clevis to any handy vehicle equipped with a trailer hitch.
The deluxe hose cart is complete with several reels of stout
hose, a number of axes and a tool chest containing extra
nozzles.

The bed of the narrow-gauge railroad that once connected
Sumpter and nearby Baker is now the grade of the excellent
blacktop road that serves the town and forest recreation
areas beyond. Sumpter is six miles south of Baker on Highway 7, then twenty miles west on Highway 220. There are
no topographic maps of the area near Sumpter, or Granite
and Whitney to the west and south, but Forest Service maps
indicate most of the important features.

Today there are 117 people living in Sumpter, but only 80
spend the winter. One place of business is in operation. A
cafe and general meeting place, it serves good coffee and
great conversation. The ranking old-timer, whose father
had lived in Sumpter since 1880, took great delight in telling me about the town. He had a storehouse of the finest
quality lies I had heard in years. He fired them out so fast
that laughter on the last interfered with the telling of the
next.

"When the town was goin' strong, there was fourteen
saloons, five hundred rah-rah girls, and one tired sinner."

After several cups of coffee, we were still undecided as to
how we might best preserve the facts as to "what old Sumpter was really like."

The rear addition to the schoolhouse has been removed and the bell has been vandalized. Built in 1888, it was last used as a city hall.

GRANITE, OREGON

Once inhabited by five thousand lively souls, the town of Granite now is best known as the smallest incorporated town in the world. With a population of one, its smallness cannot be exceeded, only equaled.

Ote Ford became the sole resident of Granite when the mayor hung himself, and "Cliff the Prospector" went looking for gold in Ten Cent Creek. Being his own mayor, council, treasurer and constituency, Ote was quick to state that Granite had a Republican administration. In the August 26, 1964, issue of the *Capitol Journal,* Ote is quoted—"There's no such thing as isolation. Too many people want to share it with you."

There are a number of reasons why people are drifting back to Granite. Easily accessible—just fifteen miles west of Sumpter—and buried deep in the beautiful Blue Mountains, the setting alone is attraction enough. Taxes are non-existent, water fees are one dollar a month, and the town treasury is in the black. At last report, the balance was more than one hundred dollars.

The Granite Mercantile displayed a fancy, rounded roof, which was later modernized to accommodate the horseless carriage trade.

The old drugstore on the left is now a seasonal dwelling. The building with the corner door was the freight office. The photograph was taken from the boardwalk in front of the Mercantile.

Although the summer population has soared to nearly one dozen, the permanent year-round count of residents remains at the minimum—one!

A few years ago the "pride of Granite"—the three-story deluxe hotel—burned to the ground. Still standing are a number of old buildings dating from the 1800's when Granite was in its prime. The small schoolhouse—later used as a city hall—has developed a decided slant. Built on a strongly sloped hill, it leans to the high side in overcompensation.

Main Street, in spite of fire and depredation, leaves the impression of being lined with stores. Prominent on a corner of the main intersection is the old Mercantile, which

*A dance floor occupied the entire upper level. The lower floor had
multiple uses—saloon, boardinghouse, and community hall.*

later became an entertainment hall and did final service as
a gas station and general store. Across the street, the drugstore—now converted to a vacation home—displays a broad-
palmed set of moose antlers on its porch roof. Next to it is
the freight office with its stylish cater-cornered doorway.
A block east are the remains of the fancy two-story dance
hall. Only the front portion of the second floor is left. The
windows have long been paneless, but the fancy sill work
and gussied shingles offer a suggestion of yesterday's
grandeur.

One general store is now in business. Strictly a seasonal
operation, it offers a warm welcome, cool refreshment, and
enchanting history.

The dusty main street passes close by the remaining homes of Whitney. Some of the outbuildings display painstaking pin and dowell construction.

WHITNEY, OREGON

Surrounded by booming gold camps, but unblessed by even token amounts of the precious metal, the town of Whitney could offer only a supporting role. The railroad that passed through town was kept busy hauling lumber to the camps and bringing gold out. Freightering and lumbering promised the town only temporary life. Its longevity depended upon two expendables, gold and timber.

Whitney was the prime station of the famous eighty-mile-long narrow-gauge Sumpter Valley Railroad. Centrally located between the two end terminals—Prairie City and Baker—it was the ideal spot for roundhouse and crews' quarters. In spite of the fourteen rail crews quartered in Whitney, and the lumber mill that employed up to seventy-five men, the population of the town never climbed much beyond one hundred. When the sawmill burned in 1918, the town became nearly deserted. A brief five-year revival occurred in 1939 when the Oregon Lumber Company rebuilt the mill in order to harvest a newly purchased block of timber.

Whitney may be reached by ten miles of passable dirt road extending south of Sumpter, or by sixteen miles of the

same kind of road extending northeast from Highway 7
near Bates. Whitney occupies only a small part of a large
grassy flat, and the dirt road does not widen appreciably as
it passes through town. "Town" is now a mere handful of
buildings, perhaps twelve or fourteen, mostly on the north
side of the street. The old roundhouse and depot are dis-
appointingly absent. Even the rails have been torn up for
scrap.

But the old sawmill is there—its proud image faithfully
reproduced in the quiet waters of the log pond. The mill
rests in the center of its own broad flat, lush with flowers
in full bloom. Knee-high purple blossoms stand uniformly
a half foot higher than yellow blossoms. I bent down to inspect an old saw blade, and the field turned from purple to
golden yellow, then returned as I regained my original per-
spective.

The mill is gutted of machinery. There is no floor, and
water seeping in from the log pond has turned the dirt to
mud a foot deep. You can navigate through the building
only by hopping from old board to rock to concrete pillar.

*Residences fronting the main street of Whitney show evidence of past
pride. Paint may fade and windowpanes may break, but vines
still beautify the porch, growing fuller with the years.*

This marvelous old sawmill is the home of a multitude of swallows.
Mill and log pond have been undisturbed for thirty-five years.

Thousands of swallows have made the old structure their
home. They resent any intrusion and take issue with
each sudden movement. Assuredly, they are harmless, but
in such great numbers they are distinctly unsettling. A simple wave of the arm, and a multitude of birds take wing.
A symphony of motion flows, at first away, and then toward
the offender. The noise rises to a peak, each bird encour-
aging the other, then settles down to a flutter of wings as
a transitory calm again prevails.

Surely great events have transpired in Whitney, but for
now its primary claim to greatness is its magnificent bird-
house standing on its own reflection, centered in a field of
purple and gold.

GALENA, OREGON

The roots of trees, downed by high winds, had levered up fantastic chunks of gold. Cleansed by rain, they glowed dully, awaiting discovery. In 1862, a group of miners made the find of their lives. They kept their secret for more than a year while they skimmed the richest deposits. By 1864 the word leaked out. "Nuggets big as your fist!" This time the wild rumors were true! Gold was sprinkled along the Middle Fork of Day River and up Elk Creek. It ran from fine

The original road can be seen disappearing downhill into the heavy brush that inundates the remaining buildings of Galena's business district.

*The old store was converted to a gas station, complete with
a single stall for drive-in service. Note the pump
handle for refilling the pump reservoir.*

to five-pound chunks. Claims were filed and the rich deposits along the Elk and the Middle Day were soon taken.

Some miners objected to claims laid out lengthwise along the stream, and forced a maximum width rule on the offenders. Each man could have a slice of stream as wide as he could reach with his pick, without moving his feet. Tall miners with long-handled picks had a distinct advantage. Later, at a meeting of five hundred miners, a standard width of fifty feet was set.

Soon two communities sprang up. One near the junction of the two streams, another about two miles north, up narrow Elk Creek Canyon. The lower camp was originally named Susanville, and had its own post office. Shortly after 1900, some miners from the upper Elk Creek camp slipped into town and stole the post office—boxes, ink pad, canceling stamp, and all. The Elk Creek camp then became Susanville, and "Old Susanville" petitioned for and received a new post office with the name of Galena. By that time much of the gold was gone, and the most likely future for the newly christened Galena seemed to be in the mining of galena, a shiny sulphide of lead.

The town of Galena never was very large, since most miners preferred to camp on their claims. Its stores came near outnumbering its residences. Lee On ran a Chinese store. Ralph Rider operated the livery and hotel. There were a dance hall and meat market, along with a number of saloons. Galena was a going town, but gold is soon gone and the miners leave with it.

A new lease was given to the life of Galena when dredges designed originally to be used on the Panama Canal were refitted and shipped in during the thirties. Reassembled, they processed much of the gravel along the Middle Fork of the John Day River, extracting gold that had eluded the miners of an earlier day. The new effort was lucrative but short-lived. The town became so quiet that in 1943 the post office was closed by request of the postmaster.

The road to Galena is long, yet pleasantly scenic. From the twin cities of John Day and Canyon City, U.S. Highway 26 extends about twenty-two miles northeast to Bates Junction. A left turn at Bates puts you through town, across the "Middle Day" River, and past the sawmill. Twenty miles on downstream are the quiet remains of Galena. The *Susanville, Oregon, 15 minute topographic map* shows the locations of both Galena and Susanville, as well as many of the mines in the area.

At Galena, several old residences and two stores line the south side of the road. The stores are deeply imbedded in tall weeds. One place of business was converted later to a combination garage and gas station. Its old pump, complete with long-handled lever, stands nearly vertical. The glass reservoir is gone, but the strip marking the level for each gallon is intact. Inside, the old one-stall garage has been converted to a meat cooler, with provisions for hanging

The staircase to this residence has been de-propped by back-scratching horses. The outside door to the attic is nearly invisible, giving the steps the illusion of leading nowhere.

freshly killed game. A single flower grows tall through a one-inch hole bored in the floor.

A metal-roofed clapboard cabin once sported an outside stairway to the attic. Recently the staircase has been dislodged by horses that graze on tall grass once worn short by frantic activity.

One family lives in Galena now, and even they find it difficult to believe that at one time five thousand miners visited town to cast their votes in a vain effort to beat out Canyon City in the contest for county seat.

SUSANVILLE, OREGON

Two miles northeast of Galena, up the narrow canyon of Elk Creek, are the sparse remains of Susanville, once called "Upper Camp." Established in 1864 as a gold camp, it received its present name in 1901 when miners lifted the post office from the rival camp downstream.

Placer deposits were rich along the two miles of canyon, and claims were narrow and lucrative. Nuggets ran large. Jane Erickson reported in the *Sunday Oregonian Magazine*

Early-morning light, filtering down the canyon, throws tall shadows on the old stamp mill at Susanville.

that a nugget large as a flatiron and worth fourteen hundred dollars was found there in 1913. It is now on display at the bank in Baker, Oregon.

Placering paid off along the entire length of Elk Creek Canyon. One of the larger outfits was owned by a Mr. Haskell. His hydraulic operation netted $165,000 in one day, and reportedly resulted in a total yield of nearly two million in gold, in spite of the ever-present loss due to high-grading. High-grading was the quasi-respectable practice of quietly pocketing the richest ore samples. Mineowners commonly paid low wages and tacitly permitted high-grading.

There was outright thievery, too, but most thieves found it difficult to leave town with the goods. Early one morning, Haskell's Chinese night watchman was observed walking down the road, suitcase in hand. The suitcase sagged heavily from its handle, and the Chinaman stopped frequently to rest. During one pause, Haskell's men rushed up and demanded the suitcase be opened. Out rolled a number of golden nuggets, the largest worth twelve hundred dollars!

Quartz prospecting began in Elk Canyon about 1869. Early samples were processed in the Cabel panamalgamation unit. Later a ten-stamp mill was built, primarily to process the ores from the nearby Badger Mine. A number of shafts found and exploited the mother lode. There were the Bull of the Woods, the Gem, the Present Need, and the Poor Man that made several men rich.

Susanville had but one street. The canyon was too narrow to provide a second. More than a thousand miners were known to crowd into town on Saturday night! White's Store was busy. So busy that to make change quickly, all prices were rounded to the nearest quarter. Anything that sold for less than fifteen cents was free.

The remains of Susanville are strung out for nearly a mile, and are now mostly empty homesites, and scattered piles of rotting timber. At the west end of town there is an old log cabin, its walls leaning under a collapsed roof. Central in town is the old mill, erect and plumb, but nearly devoid of shingles. Its machinery is gone and the trees have grown close alongside. The tar-papered cabin just opposite the mill has eight rooms and three stoves. One of the last residents strung a long antenna to improve his radio reception. He used whatever wire was handy, and what was handy was barbed wire.

This old residence, probably once a store, has eight rooms,
three stoves, and a barbed-wire radio antenna.

At the upper end of town stands a small but intact stamp
mill. Of fairly recent vintage, it has a driveway leading to
the upper end where ore can be dumped. In operation, a
reciprocating engine provided power, and a lever gave control over the flow of ore to the stamps. A stamp is merely

A three-stamp custom mill, a part of second-generation Susanville.
Note the two white boards with metal handles. When in place,
they hold two of the heavy stamps in the "up" position,
permitting one-stamp operation on small samples.

an iron rod about two inches in diameter and ten feet long.
The lower section is broadened to a width of six inches.
Each stamp weighs several hundred pounds and has, near
its upper end, a projection that allows it to be lifted. When
released, the stamp falls on the ore, crushing it fine, freeing
the particles of gold. The stamp butt was of stout metal
and high-sided to permit stamping in a bath of mercury.
The mercury amalgamated with the gold, holding it in the
bath while the worthless rock spilled over the sides.

An occasional camper or sightseer may travel up the canyon. A few stubborn prospectors still cast about for some
lost vestige of gold. Down below, a mechanized gold washing operation is reworking old gravel. But the narrow canyon is quiet. Skinners driving twelve-mule jerkliners no
longer fight the rear teams over the trace to make a tight
switchback. Welcome would be the sound of cuss words well
chosen from the vocabulary of large experience and delivered with unwavering conviction.

OREGON AREA 2

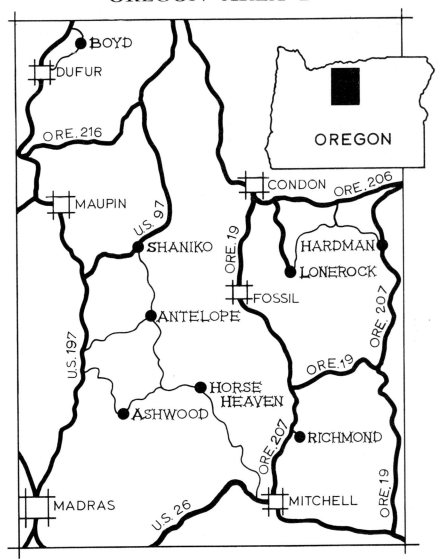

RICHMOND, OREGON

THE CLOSEST TOWN was twenty miles away and not much
when you got there. The farmers and ranchers were tired
of losing so much time commuting for supplies. A meeting
was called, ideas were set forth, and solutions were reached.
First they would build a school, then a store, and finally

Long deserted but still handsome is Richmond's little Methodist
Church. An early-morning sun paints the east side
with a momentary coat of white.

*The first building constructed in Richmond was the schoolhouse.
Pride in the new town was evident in the corner
porch and the enclosed crawl space.*

a church. The homes and entertainment halls would follow naturally. The plan was sound and the town had a
guaranteed future. But unknown to the planners, the guar-
antee would last only until the advent of the automobile.
Miles would then be measured in minutes instead of days,
and the town's reason for existence would be lost. Richmond, born in 1890, grew in a few decades to respectability,
then faded slowly again to nothing.

Highway 207, an all-weather road which is partially black-
topped, passes within a mile of Richmond. The *Richmond,
Oregon, 15 minute topographic map* is a help in locating the
town, but shows little that is not readily detected when on
the site.

The schoolhouse—first structure built, and probably one
of the last in use—is equipped with the standard bell tower
plus a covered porch on two sides. The large single class-
room is still dominated by a large black heater bearing the
name "The Smith System." A major engineering break-

Five feet high and four feet in diameter,
this old heater was said to be safe to the
touch. The actual burning compartment
is much smaller and centered within
the bulky jacket.

through for its time, it had a large flue that drew cold air
from floor level and delivered it to the chimney.

The open door of the Methodist Church invites the visitor.
A fetching alcove empties into the sanctuary where two
pews still face the empty platform. The bell tower was
vented, and probably held a bell capable of sending its call
throughout the town.

The boardinghouse—store—residence—saloon—post office building—was a forerunner to the modern enclosed shopping center. The "mall" was a covered porch that serviced
the full length of the structure.

Several large homes stand on the hill to the northwest of
town. One home is occasionally occupied and has posted on
its door a passionate plea by its owner, stating in part:
"This is not an abandoned home and is not locked—so don't
break the windows or kick in the door." ". . . Everything
worth stealing has already been stolen."

An early forerunner of the modern shopping center included a post office, boardinghouse, general store, and, of course, a mall to protect customers from excessive exposure to the elements.

Then an addendum is added: "Please, folks, if you gotta go—be brave—and use the convenient sagebrush—our water is turned off and the stool won't flush - - - - -"

Thoughtfully, owner Rod Donnelly adds a word of caution concerning rattlesnakes and exposed portions of the anatomy.

Beyond Donnelly's house, and up the hill, stands a more pretentious structure. Vacant and open to the elements, it exudes an aura of mystery. If it isn't haunted, it ought to be. Every room on the second floor is covered with old clothing. Several feet deep in most places, it offers delightful shelter to mice and other rodents. Their rustlings from under foot keep one on the alert. Occasionally an animal will scurry out on the roof and create a new sound not quickly identified. Occasional screeching sounds are probably loose

Filigreed fascia casts scalloped shadows on the weathered siding. A multitude of rodents have found a home among the litter of old clothing strewn throughout the interior.

sheets of metal roofing scraping raw edges. The stairs creak three steps ahead of your feet. The house groans—but it is old, and the wind has picked up. Weather is making, and biscuit clouds are overhead. Precursors of tornadoes, their ominous presence adds the final touch of ghostliness to the house on the hill.

The lone rock is larger than Lonerock's Methodist Church

LONEROCK, OREGON

Never was a town more appropriately named! The huge lone rock is the only dominant feature of an otherwise flat valley. Not only the town, but the stream and the valley derived their names from the impressive landmark.

A helpful gentleman in Spray, Oregon, had described the rock as "big as a house," and also firmly declared the town had recently burned to the ground. He was wrong on both counts. The town was quite intact, and the rock was not just "big as a house," it was "bigger than a church!"

The Baptists were the first to build a church in Lonerock. Soon it proved too small for the community and in 1898 a new church was planned. Times had changed. The majority

A tiny Baptist church was the first house of worship built in Lonerock.
The Dutch door, balcony, and fancy skirt were added later
when the building was converted to a residence.

of citizens were Methodist, and a Methodist Church could be built in only one place. Built stoutly and planted firmly by the rock, one must assume that Peter was quoted often, and that "Rock of Ages" echoed frequently within its walls.

Lonerock may be approached from Condon, Oregon, by proceeding east on Highway 206 for five miles, then branching to the right on an undesignated blacktop road. After

Lonerock's deserted main street. From the left: remains of a dance hall, false-fronted pastime, post office and store, and a pump without a station.

Silent swings front a school-house recently decapitated. The bell cupola once extended a dozen feet above the roof.

about fifteen miles, the road becomes gravel, and promptly slants down the steep valley wall to Lonerock. There are no topographic maps available for this portion of Oregon. Luckily, many of the towns in this unit are shown on ordinary state highway maps.

Sixteen people live in town, and the ranking resident is declared "mayor" by acclamation. Edith Perry, aged seventy-nine, holds the office at present, and is highly respected by the citizenry. The mayor pointed out some of the sites in town, occasionally throwing in a little Chamber of Commerce pitch. "Yes, that old flat thing there is the dance floor—had a building over it but we had to tear it down cause it was aleanin'. . . . The building next to it was a pastime." I asked about the name of the store. "No name—just a pastime—sold soft drinks and candy and nuts. Had a confectionery over there." Mayor Edith pointed to a small building nearly overgrown with trees. "The school is being torn down. Some people in Portland own it now. Was built in 1903 and we even had a high school on the second floor—had fifteen students."

I asked about local taxes and learned that five dollars a month was adequate to run the town.

"And we make improvements, too. We have a new water system. Ran a pipe from the spring up on the hill and the water comes down just a flyin'. No, we don't have a fire chief, but we are all members of the Fire Department. Saloons?—sure we had some. Could stir 'em with a spoon they was so thick! We graveled the streets last year and still have money left—only town in the state that's out of debt."

I left town via the gravel road to the north. The local two-wire telephone line parallels the road for a number of miles. Never had I seen a telephone system with such personality. Mayor Edith had termed it a "private line that works sometimes." Most poles were nothing but small saplings. Some were bent nearly double by the weight of the wires. At times the insulators were nailed to fence posts, or the wires merely tied with twine to a handy tree. Here and there the lines crossed and touched one another. What appeared to be an old rake handle was tied to a metal fence post, thereby gaining the rigidity needed to support the wires. At intervals, rocks as big as cabbages were hung on the line to prevent wind whipping.

The easygoing attitude that prevailed in Lonerock seemed

*Stairway to nowhere. The razing of the old hotel has ceased
momentarily, leaving a picturesque remnant.*

to stretch out along the pleasantly haphazard strands. Occasional creosoted poles appeared, then became frequent. Disgustingly upright and too perfectly aligned, they pinched to nothing the last quiet memory of Lonerock.

ASHWOOD, OREGON

The little weathered building with its corner-mounted double doors and fancy half-circle entrance porch gives little indication of its rowdy history. Called "McCallum's Saloon," it was established in 1897, two years before the town was platted. Thirty years later it suffered the insult of being placed permanently on the wagon when the Baptists converted it to a church.

Many of Ashwood's buildings have been put to new uses. Others have drifted into decay or met destruction by fire. The country store-gas station was once the hotel, with attached saloon. A house deeply buried among lofty trees was the town's favorite eating house. The Ash Butte Grange Hall is unchanged and unused. Cows graze on the lawns and wander about the streets. An old deserted store has wire mesh fencing nailed to its porch posts to prevent damage by cattle.

The road to Ashwood leads east from U.S. Highway 97 about two miles south of Willowdale. After fifteen miles of unmarked hairpin turns, the road enters the valley of Trout Creek, makes a left turn at the Baptist Church, and promptly becomes the main street of Ashwood.

I was in town less than ten minutes when I was informed, "Mrs. Allison wants to see you." The invitation was issued rather firmly by a soft-spoken but stoutly constructed man in miner's clothes. With little delay, we adjourned to the two-story deeply shaded home of Mrs. Allison. The welcome was warm, and yet strange. . . .

"How are you? I saw you enter town two days ago."

I expressed my puzzlement and she explained, "I see things—visions if you wish. I saw a tall man with dark-rimmed glasses entering town."

The miner offered corroboration. Shortly, two other miners—the Mosley brothers—joined us and formed a larger chorus of agreement. My comment that I put little faith in fortune-telling, was accepted calmly and I was treated to a recounting of past forecasts proven true, each accompanied by much head bobbing.

The three miners and the clairvoyant had been hired to look into an old mine in the area, and search out its hidden deposits. With the added power of vision, it was to be a cinch. I asked why they hadn't already located the vein, and was told that success would come soon. Word had come down from the other world to be patient.

The Baptist Church of Ashwood was originally a saloon

They were very interesting and helpful people, and their coffee was great. One of the Mosley brothers suggested that I visit Horse Heaven, and he gave me a description of the extensive remains there. This was great news, because it appeared to be a little-known site, and so far my efforts in Oregon had turned up only well-documented ghost towns.

On the heels of the suggestion that I visit Horse Heaven came the forecast "that's where you are going early tomor-

*An old country store unsuccessfully attempted modernization. The
fence running from pillar to post protects the property from
the cattle that roam freely through the town.*

row morning." I asked the seer if she would trace my future
route—it would save me a lot of map study. It seemed "the
old people" hadn't informed her of my plans more than one

*Trees grow, houses fade, and old towns are soon deep in shade.
Shown are two of the old residences on the north
side of the creek in Ashwood.*

day in advance. My impulse was to drive immediately to
Horse Heaven and prove her forecast wrong, but the light
was right for pictures in Ashwood, and there was a local
old-timer I wanted to visit.

Eighty-five-year-old Aaron Hale lives in a long trailer
pulled close to one of Ashwood's old stores. Besides Aaron
and his wife, the trailer holds three cats and a Chihuahua.
The dog is the smallest of the lot. He thinks he is a cat
and gets along fine. All six evidenced a warm welcome, and
soon Aaron was telling about old Ashwood.

He remembered best the humorous events like the time
the men at King Mine quit. "There were seventy men working shifts, living in a big boardinghouse up there. Had a

gal hired to run it and cook—she did for quite a while—then quit. Tired of being unappreciated. They hired two men to take over. For supper they served oyster stew and crackers. The next mornin' they dished up hot cakes and syrup, and you could roll up the cakes like a cigarette, then throw 'em—they'd open up and fly like a pigeon. The boys threw 'em all, then threw out the table—and then the chairs—and all walked to Ashwood to the cafe." Aaron pointed to a dilapidated old building a few lots away. The superintendent returned and found the mine shut down and the men in town. They would go back to work if he got a new cook— he did—two women. Really turned out the ore for a while !"

Aaron had a friend named Tom Brown, who had his own claim, but had to work to earn dynamite money. His claim lapsed as he was comin' close, and old Hubbard filed on it —Tom took him to court and got it back—turned out a good mine, too.

"Ashwood had its heydey," says Aaron. "There were three hundred people here in the nineties—and now there's just four." He didn't count the folks doing temporary exploration work. "The Hamilton Hotel had ten rooms—and the town had its own paper, the *Ashwood Prospector*." He dug out an old copy dated May 4, 1901. Half of the front page was an ad asking people to come live in Ashwood. A Justice of the Peace announced in a box ad, "Careful attention given collections." Much of the paper was filled with ads from the nearby and larger town of Antelope. In fact, the *Ashwood Prospector* was printed in Antelope.

From the beginning, Ashwood had been overshadowed by Antelope. When mining activity began to slow down, shortly after 1900, it was logical for those out of work to seek employment in Antelope. Soon stores were closing down for lack of business. A small flurry of mining raised hopes momentarily in 1925. During the thirties and forties, the town revived somewhat in response to mercury mining at Horse Heaven, twenty miles or so to the east.

Things are quiet these days in Ashwood. There are more cows in town than people. It is a relaxing place to visit, and a restful place to camp.

I overnighted by the old grange building in the center of town, and was awakened early by cattle rubbing vigorously against the tailgate of my truck. Soon I had breakfasted, and in accordance with the seer's forecast, was on my way to Horse Heaven.

Typical board-and-batten home in Horse Heaven. Area is mainly scrub, sand, and rattlesnakes.

HORSE HEAVEN, OREGON

Two old prospectors, Champion and Kenton, first located the fine particles of red cinnabar on the divide between Cherry Creek and Muddy Creek. The find developed into a major producer of mercury.

That is the way one historical account disposed of the story behind Horse Heaven. But the real story is fantastic, and perhaps never before told in its entirety. It was related to me by a tall, somewhat graying gentleman now prospecting at Horse Heaven. His name is Ray R. Whiting, Jr., and he, more than any other man, knows the total story—because he lived it.

"Old Champion was a great prospector—could find it as if he could smell it. Always scratching though—like he had the seven-year itch and no bath. He used to take some of

Loading tipple, long unused, had space beneath to position vehicle for loading. Two hundred million pounds of cinnabar ore were pulled from the hill at the left. Crushed and roasted it released one million pounds of liquid mercury.

us kids along with him. One summer my buddy, Harry Hoy, and myself were out here camping and prospecting with our dads. Old Champion was along, and he was showing Harry and me the float of cinnabar that he had found earlier."

We walked a few steps over to the scant shade of a juniper tree. Ray bent down and picked up a handful of whitish granules that covered the area.

"This is the stuff. In fact it was right here that Champion panned some out to show us."

Rather than just talk about it, Ray got a pan and a plastic jug filled with water and proceeded to pan the sample. Quickly the coarse chunks went over the rim of the pan. More water, and the finer granules were slopped over the edge. In moments Ray had the original handful down to a small residue of deep red powder and black sand.

"There—you see the red—that's cinnabar—mercury sulfide—and it's mostly mercury. Well, old Champion had found the stuff earlier the same year—that was 1933—but had given up on it because it was just float—stuff that washed in. Being on top of a divide, he figured it couldn't be much and told us it was worthless. Like any other kids, we figured a big lode was nearby, so we got to looking around. Found some outcrops that looked good, so we started digging."

Ray pointed out the spot a few yards up the slope. "Spent most of the summer. Brought supplies in and made a project out of it. Harry and I tunneled for sixty days. That's sticking pretty good for a couple of high-school kids, but we were beginning to lose our confidence. Eating lunch one day, we were sitting by the tunnel, and I got to kicking at a rock— just messing around. That rock just flipped over. It was wet on the bottom and bright red!"

We looked at some samples that Ray had nearby—pink tracings went everywhere throughout the pale whitish rock.

"Here—look see how it comes to life when you wet it." Ray poured some water on the rock, and each pink line became flaming red. "We started a new tunnel, and in a couple of days we were really in it—solid cinnabar, and slimy with beaded mercury. Our dads had us sit on the claim and we formed a company. Us kids got a third interest for making the find. Later when we sold out, Harry and I got 11 percent, and we were both rich."

In a few years the new Crystal Syndicate had the mine in production. Later it was named the Horse Heaven Mines,

*A jury-rigged furnace is now being used to roast
mercury from cinnabar samples.*

Inc. In 1936 the Sun Oil Company bought the mine and operated it until 1944. One hundred thousand tons of ore were
removed from deep within the hill, leaving tunnels fourteen
hundred feet long on ten different levels. The deepest over

*The mine dump threatened to inundate homes in Horse Heaven.
"Thank God, the vein ran out," stated one miner
as he packed his belongings.*

*Rock face skylined at the center of the photograph bears a likeness
to that of the man who reportedly found a rich cinnabar
outcrop, then died without relocating it.*

three hundred feet down. Four huge stopes, or caverns, were left where massive pockets of ore were removed.

A twenty-ton mill and reduction furnace turned out 15,000 flasks of mercury, each weighing seventy-five pounds, and valued at a total of seven million dollars at the old prices. The mill burned in 1946, and except for a spurt in 1954, the mining was finished.

At its peak the town had a population somewhat over a hundred. It had a post office, dozens of cabins, a few bunkhouses, one cookhouse, a few office buildings, a schoolhouse with fifteen students, and uncounted numbers of rattlesnakes. The rattlesnakes are still there. Ray killed three the day before I arrived.

No topographic maps are available for towns in the area, but Horse Heaven is easily reached by driving the fifteen miles of good gravel road extending east of Ashwood.

I asked Ray what would a rich high-school kid do with his money and his life back in 1933.

"Well—I built a fancy restaurant in California. It was a dandy—and lots of famous people used to come there. Made money, too. But somehow I let it all slip through my fingers."

"Rags to riches to rags again," I volunteered.

"No, more like tatters now. I'm on a project here to locate some new deposits. The government is helping out, since the need for mercury is critical."

There was more to the story, and Ray led the way to a spot where we could look at a skylined outcrop.

"See that rock up there? Looks just like a man's head, doesn't it? See the open mouth? That looks just like a dear old friend of mine. I was with him when he died, and he looked just like that rock. He had the same nose and chin."

I agreed that the rock certainly looked like an old man's final profile.

"He told be before he died that he and a pal of his—way back in '35—had been kicking around just west of the old cookhouse. That's about where we are standing now. They uncovered an outcrop of cinnabar that looked redder than the one I had found. They agreed to keep it a secret, maybe try and file on it later. They never did, and he wanted me to know about it. That's why I am out here now. I intend to find that outcrop."

It has been over a year since I visited with Ray Whiting, Jr. By now he has either found the new lode or ended his search and turned Horse Heaven over to the rattlesnakes.

The Silvertooth Saloon, once a lively establishment. According to an old-timer living in nearby Ashwood, Silvertooth liked to see the saloon shot up once in a while. If the customers didn't do it, he would fire a few bullets himself.

ANTELOPE, OREGON

Supplies were needed at Canyon City. Gold had been discovered. The nearest supply point was The Dalles, and a route between the two points was quickly established. In 1862 the Wheelers built a way station at a point sixty miles

Built immediately after the great fire of 1898, this fraternal hall housed the offices of the "Antelope Herald" on its ground level.

*An aborted building effort, recently abandoned, drew this comment
from one resident: "Ain't much for looks but
it's sure hell for stout!"*

out of The Dalles. They named it Antelope. Soon Nathan
Wallace built a store, then a smithy and stockade were
added. Competitors built on a better site two miles north,
and all of Antelope soon moved to "New Antelope."

Immediately the Union House Hotel was constructed.
Soon a large livery and dance hall named "Tamany" was
built. There was no stockade at the new town, even though

Indian threats continued. F. W. Silvertooth, operator of a saloon bearing his name, is said to have "saved the day" when the regular stage driver refused the run because of Indian danger. The stage operators were so happy to have Silvertooth volunteer that they offered him generous payment. "Just name your price."

"Well," answered Silvertooth, "just give me some Saw Log and some Battle Axe."

Armed with these two most popular brands of plug tobacco, the intrepid Silvertooth whipped the teams up and dusted the stage out of town. His plan was simple. Each time Indians were sighted, he stopped the stage, waved them in, and handed out presents.

In spite of Indian problems, the town grew rapidly, and in 1887, according to H. C. Roper, "It was visible to the naked eye." By 1896 there were one hundred seventy folk, three saloons, a bowling alley, and several churches. Two years later the town burned. Many residences and all but one building on Main Street went up in smoke. But Antelope was an important place, and it quickly rebuilt, even larger than before.

John Silvertooth, son of the one-time stage driver, is presently living in a shaded bungalow at the north edge of Antelope. John and his wife Laura remember what Antelope was like at the turn of the century. Laura began, "Why, yes, it was the main stop 'tween The Dalles and Canyon City, and a big sheep shipping point. The population reached two thousand at one time. There were three hotels, three stores, a rooming house—"

Then John chimed in. "Three, no, four saloons—Doyles, Macbeths, and Silvertooths. That was my father's place. Then there was one more—two smithies and a couple of red-light places. There was a madam and two girls at the one place—"

Laura helped out on the names, "Pearl and Flossy—Flossy was the fat one."

John volunteered, "Pearl got sick—appendix. The doc operated in the drugstore. That Pearl, she was good-looking —red hair—real nice looking."

Laura added, "They buried one of them in our cemetery. At first they were against it, but finally they decided to put her in a lonely corner, where she couldn't do any harm."

In 1900 the railroad reached Shaniko, a small town eight miles north of Antelope. It became an important railhead

The Methodist church, built in 1898 but unused in recent years, is still complete, right up to the bell in the tower. A small brick community church a block away now serves the area's needs.

and lured away most of Antelope's major businesses and professional men. The population shrank, and most of the stores on Main Street became vacant. Numerous fires ravaged the unoccupied buildings. A pitifully small portion of Antelope remains standing today. The old Methodist Church, a fraternal hall, Silvertooth's Saloon, and scattered residences offer evidence of Antelope's more active moment in history.

Just as Antelope had drawn heavily on Ashwood, so Shaniko subtracted the life from Antelope. But Shaniko was to prosper only briefly, then suffer a similar fate.

The Shaniko Hotel had heat in every room. Retired sheepmen congregate here to tell stories and watch the strange antics of tourists.

SHANIKO, OREGON

Bankers in The Dalles decided that the riches from the large wool-growing area to the south could best be tapped by railroad. Called the Columbia Southern Railroad, it branched off the main line at Biggs on the Columbia River, and in 1900 reached the site of the old Cross Hollows Stage Station and Post Office. The station had been operated from 1874 to 1877 by a German immigrant named August Scherneckau. The Indians trusted Herr Scherneckau in spite of the wide difference in backgrounds and the resulting com-

Built in 1902 of unique architecture, the schoolhouse had an eight-sided combination entrance, cloakroom, and bell tower. The flagpole seems to have been an afterthought.

munications problem. Neither could twist his tongue around the sounds favored by the other. August used the rolling r-r-r-r and broad guttural vowels of his homeland. The Indians returned each word with lighter vowels and evenly valued syllables. Thus Scherneckau became Shaniko, and Shaniko was the name chosen for the new post office established at the railhead.

Quickly a "town of permanence" was built. A large, brick two-story hotel was raised. It was plush, with heat available in every room. Chimneys stand out of the roof at close intervals. The corner porch is broad, fully balustraded, and supported by white-painted columns.

Across from the hotel a row of stores catered to the

mixed trade, supplying the wants of sheepherders and railroad men alike. A fancy two-story firehouse served also as a meeting place for the town council. A school was erected from funds donated, and taxes paid for an elaborate water system. Shaniko had grown up to be a fancy town, but it possessed some earthy problems.

Somewhere in history, "shepherd" became "sheepherder," and much of the attendant respect fell away. Cowmen hated them, and mothers feared them. In defense of their daughters, the women of Shaniko tolerated an elaborate red-light district. Shaniko had thirteen establishments, mostly referred to kindly as "sporting houses."

Less than a dozen years ago, the town was just a small deserted shipping point. Then a few newspapers carried stories about the "quaint and quiet place." Tourists arrived in large numbers and left with amazing quantities of "artifacts." At first the people of Shaniko objected to such invasion and were insulted to have their town classified as a ghost. But there was a new future for Shaniko now, a showplace for the local history, and a watering place for a new kind of sheep. The new variety was similar to the original, varying mostly in eating habits, consuming much in the way of pop, hot dogs, and Kodak film.

Tattered but comfortable lounging sofas, and hard-backed benches line the side of the hotel where the porch offers shade and view. Old-timers, mostly retired sheepherders, make frequent use of these comforts. Each seems to have a favored spot from which he can eye passing tourists from under lowered brim. A notably ugly wooden Indian stands guard at the hotel door, viewing visitors with a like reserve.

The schoolhouse at the north edge of town displays a unique architecture. Built in 1902, it is fronted by a tall ventilated octagonal tower. A flagpole extends from its upper portion at an angle a bit up from horizontal. The building is large and square, its roof slanting from all sides to a flat top. Traces of boardwalk still front the school and skirt the dusty street. The few children in Shaniko now travel by bus to the school at Maupin, thirty-three black-topped miles away.

A few blocks west of the old school, a large rectangular structure dominates the sky. Resembling the base of some giant windmill, it would place in awe the bravest Don Quixote. Inspection shows it to be a deluxe large-capacity water tower. Water tanks occupy the upper levels, and

*Overflow pipe on water tank extends well out from eave to give excess
water a free drop to the ground. The unusual size of the tower
and tanks offers a clue to the magnitude of once-busy Shaniko.*

pipes extend downward. Below frostline they branch in
multiple directions.

The school and the hotel both indicate that Shaniko was
once a much larger town than is evident today. But to
justify the large water tower, one must mentally fill in the
empty lots that extend for blocks in all directions, and replace the absent stores on the intersecting main streets.

With a little imagination, one can hear the old eight
wheeler whistling at the mile marker, and see the flock of
sheep top the rise above town.

*The beauty of sunburst gables on the outside matched that of rainbows
cast inward by windows of stained glass. This was once
one of the finer homes of Boyd, Oregon.*

BOYD, OREGON

Fifteen Mile Creek carried water enough to power a mill,
and wheat fields extended for miles in every direction. It
was a proper place to build a gristmill and granary. A
little store half a mile north of the creek crossing had been
built in 1870. When the mill was constructed some thirty
years later, the store suddenly found itself the center of a
booming community. Homes were built, the store was enlarged, and a blacksmith moved in to set up shop. Stories
vary as to the existence of a hotel in Boyd. Some claim
there was just a boardinghouse, which has since burned
down. Others claim the old house at the south edge of
town was used as a hotel for a time. Half a dozen fancy

erted granary and idle grain chute
frame the old water powered stone
roller mill of Boyd.

Millowner's residence was both the home
of the owner and entertainment center
for customers. Built solidly of rock,
it stands mid-level between the
holding pond and the mill.

Solid rubber tires, weathered and cracked, once carried heavy
loads of grain "smoother than any wagon."

homes of the nineteenth century have lasted well. Under the shade of broad-branched trees they stand, badly in need of paint, yet proudly displaying sunburst-patterned gables and stained-glass windows. Part of the original store remains and is presently in use as a storage shed, but the outstanding remains of Boyd are at the mill site, about a half mile to the south.

The town and the mill are both easily reached via a good gravel road branching east about three and a half miles north of Dufur, on U.S. Highway 197. Boyd is about one-half mile from the highway, and the mill is immediately south of town. The *Dufur East 7½ minute topographic map* shows the location of both sites.

At the mill site, waters of Fifteen Mile Creek were diverted to a holding pond. Located above the mill, with a vertical drop of sixty feet, the water rushed downward through an eighteen-inch-diameter flume to make powerful contact with a large waterwheel. Cogwheels increased the force by sacrificing speed, then delivered the power to a slowly revolving stone roller. As a boy might crush leaves by riding a bicycle in tight circles, the broad roller crushed grain against a stationary stone base. If some ground up rock was found in the flour, it merely lent a little body and character, say those who lament the present scarcity of stone-ground flour.

Against the mill lean the remains of old farm implements, wagons, and cars. One ancient truck chassis is bodyless, but its wooden-spoked, solid-rubber-tired wheels still cap the front axle.

Above the mill is a impressive three-story rock home. Occupied originally by the millowner, it served a second important purpose. Customers were entertained while their wheat was ground. Overnight stays were common. The home is occupied at present, and water that once powered the mill now sprays generously on lawn and garden.

The reason why the mill shut down and Boyd became deserted can only be speculated. Certainly a waterwheel-powered roller mill was technically behind the times shortly after the mill was constructed. Electricity was soon available and, in most mills, steel rollers replaced those of stone. Other mills could process grain for less, and consequently offer a better purchase price. And besides, with a gas-driven truck, what farmer would pass up a chance to haul his harvest to the big city, especially if the added return more than paid for a night on the town.

OREGON AREA 3

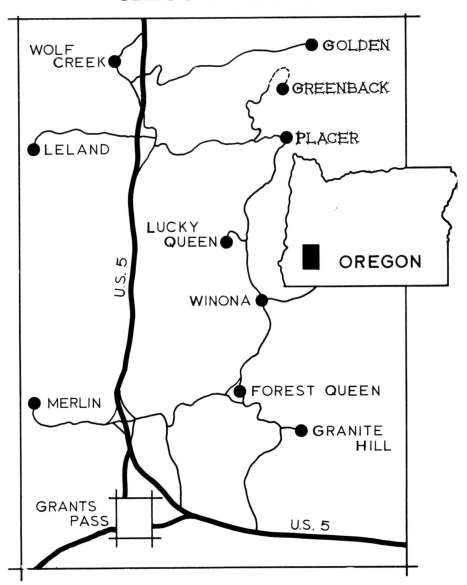

WOLF CREEK ● ● GOLDEN

● GREENBACK

● PLACER

● LELAND

LUCKY QUEEN ●

■ OREGON

WINONA ●

● FOREST QUEEN

● MERLIN

● GRANITE HILL

U.S. 5

GRANTS PASS

U.S. 5

PLACER, OREGON

PEOPLE ARE INTRIGUED by maps, especially large maps. My map of Oregon was about four by five feet, and when spread out on a cafe counter, it became an open invitation to comment. Before I could completely unfold the map, someone

This gracious old home in Placer still has washing hanging on the porch. Long since dried, the clothes are falling off in tatters.

would generally inquire as to where I had been and where I was going next. Hopefully, they would point out some little-known site that would turn out to be a ghost town worth visiting.

That is just what happened at a small coffee shop in the central Oregon town of Prineville. The waitress asked, after lifting the corner of the map to find a place for my coffee, "Have you been to Golden? I was born there, and the last time I visited the town it still had a church, some stores, and a few homes. The whole place was deserted. Used to be a mining town."

We located the town on the map to find that it was just one of a number of towns, all of which had the earmarks of long desertion. Strung out in a line, north of Grants Pass in southwest Oregon, were Granite Hill, Forest Queen, Winona, Lucky Queen, Placer, Greenback, Golden, and Speaker. It developed that three of these towns had remnants worth observing and stories worth telling, but to find the three, I had to search out all eight.

The storekeeper's residence is encroached upon by heavy brush. In a few years its collapsed remains will be covered by greenery.

The *Metsker map of Josephine County,* and the *USGS 15 minute Glendale, Oregon, topographic maps* are both of value but of little help in finding a way off the new Interstate. Turnoffs, signs, new roads—nothing agrees with the old maps until you get a few miles away from the Interstate.

A dozen miles up Louse Creek, a triangular intersection located the site of Forest Queen. Only a cabin or two remained. One cabin was occupied, and its owner was quick

to agree that the town was essentially nonexistent, and volunteered that nearby Granite Hill was the same. He was
right. Granite Hill was but a flat spot occupied by a piece
of road-building equipment.

At Winona, a few miles north, the townsite had become
the Shady Creek subdivision. Lucky Queen was merely a
mine site, and little was left. The dirt road leading north
toward Placer deteriorated quickly to mudholes, then
abruptly worsened. Boulders replaced the mud, and the
grade became steep. In places, a four-mile-per-hour crawl
was too fast.

An hour later the road leveled and broke into the open.
A few deserted cabins were sprinkled about. The sun had
set and it was rapidly darkening. A lighted window guided
me to the home of Mr. and Mrs. Howard Coome. They were
surprised at the circuitous route I had used to reach Placer,
and I was surprised to learn that I was in Placer. The
Coomes explained that the little town of Placer was across
the creek that flowed alongside their home, and that it was
not a "remote" community, but located on a blacktop highway, just four miles from the Sunny Valley Junction of Interstate 5.

In answer to a multitude of questions, the Coomes informed me that the town was largely deserted, but that it
was at one time a rather large community. They further
stated that the town was now reduced to a half-dozen or so
structures, but did have two outstanding features: an old
school and an old-timer. They thoroughly recommended a
visit to both.

The next morning I toured Placer, observing the few remaining structures along its two parallel streets, then drove
a few miles west to talk with the old-timer.

George Arlington Klonus is eighty-five years old, of German extraction, and sharper of mind and eye than most
youngsters half his age.

"Sure it was a big town—biggest in the county for a while.
Had three stores. I ran one of them from '32 to '35. Not
sure just when the town started, but it was 'way before 1900.
Had a post office up 'til '24. For a while it was mostly a
place for Blind Pigs."

I asked for an explanation, and George Arlington Klonus
patiently explained. "Speakeasies—you know—where the
back door was always open—a few girls, too. Sure sold a
lot of homemade whiskey. More than twenty stills were

The school at Placer once had twenty-four students. When the last
family with children moved away, the teacher sat
on the steps and collected her pay.

spread out along the creek. One old fellow used to put
glycerine in his moonshine to make it smoother. Found him
one day—dead—sittin' in his rocking chair!"

Mr. Klonus was Clerk of the School District for a while
—"up 'til the last family with kids moved out of town. That
was three months after school started, so the teacher just
sat on the steps and collected pay."

The lack of buildings in town puzzled me until George
explained. "Most of them burned. Set afire, we thought, by
just one guy. He was always stealing firewood—never cut
his own, and always had plenty. Had a habit of knocking
his pipe out—didn't even realize he was doing it. We know
he burned down his own cabin and three others, maybe
more."

There is an old covered bridge a mile west of George's
home. The date of construction is somewhat vague, but it

*One of Oregon's few remaining covered bridges spans Shank's Creek
a few miles below Placer, where the old Applegate
Trail makes its crossing.*

was one of the early bridges on the Applegate Trail. Rebuilt in 1925, it looks brand new. George recommended the bridge and the town of Golden as being worthy of a visit, and especially endorsed the old community of Greenback, just up the hill a ways.

"That Greenback was a fine place. The mine always had plenty of fellows wanting work there—good high-gradin' —twenty-five dollars a day easy—no trick at all to pocket a few of the best chunks—some of 'em near pure gold. No saloon there so they all came to Placer to spend it."

Speaker, the last of the string of eight towns, was quickly evaluated by George Arlington Klonus as "underwhelming." I crossed it off my list.

The foundations of the original twenty-stamp mill can be seen in the foreground in front of the more modern ball mill. The entering road is visible at top.

GREENBACK, OREGON

The mineralized stretch of ground connecting Placer, Greenback, and Golden is thickly shot with mines. The Star, Gold Cup, Yellowhorn, Jim Blaine, Martha, and even the Shot Mine, have punched deep holes in search of gold.

Ed Hanham and his partner discovered one of the richest. Called the Greenback Mine, it proved rich enough to require its own mill. The heavy metal parts for a twenty-stamp mill were hauled three miles up the steep, winding

*An ancient timber and log skid, probably used to bring in heavy
equipment for Greenback's first stamp mill.*

road extending north from Placer. When completed, it immediately went into twenty-four-hour operation and required a crew of twenty men. Cabins were built to make
work at the mill more attractive. Soon a company store was
added. In 1902, Greenback became officially a town when
a post office was authorized. It lasted only six years, but
during that time many fortunes were made.

"Everyone that worked there went away rich," stated one
former resident. The owners finally stopped all but the most
ingenious high-graders by requiring miners to change
clothes at the end of each shift.

No liquor was permitted in the company town of Greenback. The road to Placer was well worn. Miners made frequent trips to relieve the itch of money. Their horses knew
the way and often returned to stand at the hitching rail in
Greenback while drivers and passengers, unaware their
destination had been reached, continued to sleep off the
effects of their celebration.

The road to Greenback is in poor shape now. It is best
to walk the last mile as there is deep mud along the final

A stamp cam, about two feet across which once rotated on a drive shaft, lifting a heavy stamp, then permitting it to fall freely upon crushable ores. Note the worn key slot.

stretch. Heavy grout foundations, an old log skid, and a few stamp lifters are at the burned-over millsite. The stamp lifters, heavy double cams of cast metal, show the reason for their abandonment. Rectangular recesses, where locking keys once held them firmly to the driving axle, are worn to ineffectual smoothness. The shrinking evolution of the mining effort since the rich veins petered out in the early 1900's can be pieced together by observing the age and size of the ore buckets scattered about the premises.

A small ball mill has been erected next to the remains of the old mill. It has also ceased operations. Beside the mill a number of ore cars stand on rusty wheels. One car car-

An ore car at the Greenback Mine stands on trackless ground. Hopeful new ownership and subsequent abandonment are evident.

ries a comparatively fresh sign stating "Jos. Sourdoughs Co.," a name undeniably appropriate.

Adjacent to the newer mill are a few of the original mine shacks of Greenback. They are presently used for equipment storage and are securely locked. A lonely outhouse stands a short distance from the storage sheds. A continuous stream, from an artesian well, is directed under considerable pressure against the outhouse door, effectively prohibiting its use. The water then flows down the road from Greenback, transforming a dirt road to a tree-lined lane of mud—two feet deep. Far-reaching, and better than a locked gate, it prevents easy access and precludes any possibility of heavy equipment being stolen.

GOLDEN, OREGON

There was gold to be found in the gravel of Coyote Creek, but it was finely divided and thinly scattered. A man could hardly make wages panning by hand. The few miners sticking it out on Coyote Creek were quick to join the 1850 rush to the new find on the Salmon River. As the white man left, Chinese moved in to take over the deserted claims. Soon there were more than five hundred spread out along the length of Coyote Creek.

It took only a few years to skim the cream of rich deposits at the Salmon find. Soon the thin deposits at Coyote Creek began to look good by comparison, especially in the light of new placering techniques.

The Chinese were quickly run off and old claims were reoccupied. Hydraulic placering was soon tried and found profitable. The word spread and more miners came to stake claims. The community slowly grew as Coyote Creek continued to release its treasure.

There were more than 150 people living along the creek in 1892. The time had come to organize.

A "Campbellite" church was built that year. Soon a carriage house was constructed, and a general store also opened for business. In 1896 the town was formally recognized, and a post office opened under the name of "Golden."

By all reason, they should have named the town "Ruble City." The first minister was William Ruble, later replaced by his son, W. N. Ruble. Schuyler Ruble was the first postmaster, and S. C. Ruble was active in the local mining effort. He was the inventor of the Ruble elevator, a device designed to remove unwanted gravel from stream beds. S. C. Ruble also ran the general store. S. C. Ruble and Schuyler Ruble may have been the same person. If so, he was obviously talented and busy.

It must have been a red-letter day when storekeeper Ruble turned his duties over to a man named other than Ruble. The new storekeeper was Columbus Bennett. Ruble was Bennett's uncle. Later, Harold McIntosh ran the store, but of course Bennett was McIntosh's uncle.

Coyote Smith was appointed Justice of the Peace, and apparently was unrelated to the Rubles. Justice must remain aloof and untainted.

The schoolhouse was in operation about a half mile down the creek to the west. On Sundays it served as a church,

Golden's Community Church is truly a classic. Built and first used by the Campbellites, it later served as a house of worship for the Free Methodists.

with the Rev. Mark David officiating. Sinners had little chance in Golden. Two churches and no saloons. Perhaps that is why miners lived strung out down the valley.

Golden today consists of a church, carriage house, the old store, several old homes, and numerous shacks scattered

The carriage house is on the left, general store on the right. The church is buried deep in the trees at the left.

along the stream bed. It is easily reached, just four miles east of Wolf Creek on the Coyote Creek Road.

Mr. and Mrs. Orville Cornwell own much of the ghost town now, and are living in one old residence while they properly recondition another. Their future home is a handsome one and nicely intact where it was protected by a metal roof. Elsewhere it has more of an open-air motif. I stepped through a large opening in the rear porch and was immediately met by two squirrels moving at high speed and headed for the nearest tree. I stepped through a doorway into the old living room. There, to the right, was an old stove resting on a metal floor protector. Standing upon the broad metal sheet was a third squirrel. He reacted quickly, his hind legs moving faster than the smooth surface could accommodate. His speed built up slowly, and he headed toward the door, making a smooth turn to miss my feet. As he approached,

*The little school did double duty, serving as a second church each
Sunday. Golden had two churches and no saloons.*

his rear legs were beginning to slide toward the outside of his turn, but he continued without deceleration, and passed me going broadside, his rear "wheels" still spinning, his head turned sharply in the direction of the skid. His rear end was slightly ahead as he passed through the door. Then with a wobble of over-correction, he reached top speed and lined away for the nearest tree.

The Golden Community Church is a classic, ranking with those in Richmond, Oregon, and Atlantic City, Wyoming. Rebuilt in 1950, it is in excellent shape. The bell is still in its tower, but only because of a watchful neighbor.

Not long ago, when the town appeared deserted, a man drove quietly into town, parked his pickup close beside the church, and unloaded an extension ladder. The interloper proceeded to climb to the belfry, carrying a block and tackle slung across his shoulder. Unaware that he was observed, he loosened the ventilating boards. BONG! The bell rang. It rang so loud that the sound of shot and ricochet was hardly detectable. But the would-be thief knew he was in trouble. Either the hand of God was poised to strike again, or someone was shooting in his direction. He left town with little dignity and much alacrity.

Eighty-year-old Harold McIntosh, one-time operator of the general store, and long-time resident of Golden, lives a quarter mile northeast of town in Robinson's Gulch, alongside one of the finest strawberry patches in Oregon. He is a willful, honest man. He may fracture a word here and there, but the meaning is always clear. I introduced myself, and asked, "Harold McIntosh, I believe?"

With just the faintest twinkle in his eye, he replied, "Well . . . mostly." We talked strawberries and weather for a while, then got down to serious history.

Harold McIntosh mined Robinson Gulch with his own Giants (hydraulic guns), pouring out a mighty stream. Three men helped him with the operation. "We got some gold—but it wasn't so good. Not as good as Coyote Creek —they took out millions there. Used to get seventeen dollars an ounce. In 1933 it went up to thirty-five dollars. The gold was nine hundred fine."

I asked if it was true that Golden had no saloon.

"Never had a saloon, but they all draink—sort of 'no whiskey—no mining.' Never saw anyone drunk, though."

Business was good when Harold ran the store. "Had to build on a lean-to— needed more room. That was about the

This old residence, slated for reconstruction and occupation, was, at the time, the home of an active family of squirrels.

time they were tearing down some of the houses to get the gold beneath them." He paused, then grinned and went on. "Used to hold dances at the store. Church wouldn't allow it. I finally gave up and built a dance hall down at Wolf Creek. Had real good times there, but church folk still gave me trouble. Used to parade around the dance hall prayin' away the devil—was fanatakism—pure fanatakism."

The loose boards in the belfry are the result of an abortive attempt to steal the bell. The would-be thief got the surprise of his life.

PART II
WASHINGTON

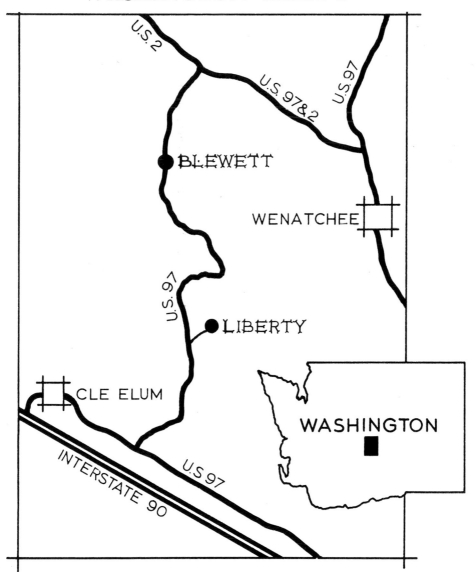

LIBERTY, WASHINGTON

THE SUN DISAPPEARED behind Teenaway Ridge on my left. Highway 97 continued to climb in broad curves. Horizons lowered as altitude was gained. The sun reappeared frequently, offering brief postponements to the day's end. The

Two young lads of Thorp, Washington, thoroughly enjoy a hot July day. The old mill pond makes a perfect swimming hole. The huge flour mill, long unused, was waterpowered as was its companion sawmill just downstream.

road leveled and the sun set for good as I pulled into Liberty Guard Station, fifteen miles northeast of Cle Elum in central Washington. A brief look at the topographic maps showed that I had passed the Liberty turnoff a quarter of a mile back. Liberty is located at the joining edges of the *Liberty and Thorp, Washington, 15 minute* maps and the maps have to be matched to make out the route. Retracing my path, I reached the turnoff and headed east up Williams Creek, enjoying occasional glimpses of quiet pools. Wind-rowed gravel banks indicated the area had been placered heavily. The last traces were the obvious result of a

A miner's cabin located across the creek from town has a shaft in the center of its floor, with a ladder extending downward. The abandoned shaft probably served as a food cooler.

dredging operation. A short two miles from the highway, the road crossed Lion Creek, angled slightly right, and suddenly became the main street of Liberty.

A sign on the left read "For Sale, Mining Claims, Cabins." There were old cabins on both sides of the street, and just visible across the valley was a string of mining shacks. My maps indicated that two tunnels and three shafts were to be found near the mine shacks. The road divided at the upper end of town. The right fork dead-ended in a quiet clearing, and I made camp for the night. Making camp was simply a matter of jockeying the truck about until two spirit levels were satisfied. The levels are mounted at right angles. One indicates fore and aft slant—the other shows my "roll attitude." I planned to do a bit of reading, so this night I parked with a quarter bubble on the left of the level to raise the head of the bed.

It was a peaceful spot. The waters of tiny Boulder Creek rushed by a few feet away. It was quite a relief to be

camped by a genuine ghost town, after suffering through
three days of high expectations and dashed hopes.

Reviewing my notes, I counted seven disappointments in
a row. First there was Maryhill, in south-central Washington. Once a going town, it had degenerated into an orchard
and truck farm. An old store stood alone among young fruit
trees. Part of two old ferries were at the banks of the Columbia River, put to disuse by a new highway bridge. On
the hill above town, a replica of England's Stonehenge
seemed strangely out of place. A few miles away, the Maryhill Museum overlooked the Columbia from a lofty perch on
the north bank. Inside were many items of interest, mostly
art objects and European royal family relics. It was a fascinating museum, but not a single item pertained to the old
town of Maryhill. Both the Stonehenge memorial and the
museum were built by Samuel Hill, a famous pioneer in road
building. I speculated as I drove away that many visitors
to the two sites must have departed with the same thought:
"What in Sam Hill?"

Thorp, one hundred miles north, had been next on the
list. Bypassed by the highway, it had shrunk, but was still
too lively to be called a ghost town. The old water-powered
flour mill at the north end of town was fascinating. Complete with kids swimming in the mill pond, it was a sight
guaranteed to transport the beholder to the time of his child-
hood. I would have joined them had I packed a swimsuit.
One of the youngsters offered the loan of his!

To the north, the towns of Easton, Cabin Creek, Lester,
Ronald and Cle Elum all warranted investigation, but
failed to fit the category of ghost towns. With mild irrita-
tion I recalled my troubles with a loud and persistent cafe
operator who ranted so continuously that no one could mount
a response. He badgered me to buy something or he
"wouldn't answer a damn question!" I ordered coffee, paid
for it, then handed it back to him with the suggestion that
he drink it, and treat the customers to a few seconds of bliss-
ful quiet.

And that reminded me of the quiet that permeated my
campsite at Liberty. I was again relaxed, anxious only for
the next day to arrive.

The morning was cool, and the skies were clear overhead.
A few puffy clouds were climbing over the hills to the west.
The conditions were ideal for photographing the old mine
shacks that extended down the south side of the valley. The

Numerous shafts near this shack were covered by rotting timbers forming unintentional traps for unwary visitors. The sagging floor of the cabin gave off a hollow sound, indicating shaft work below.

Repaired, rebuilt, and adapted to changing times and varying fortune, this cabin at the east end of Liberty has been "recently" sided with narrow clapboards rejected as waste from a nearby sawmill.

first cabin was securely locked with a hasp of unique construction. A large saw blade, hinged at one end, spanned the
entire width of the door. A square hole, obviously burned
through with a cutting torch, allowed a U-bolt to be exposed
far enough for a gigantic padlock to pass through its eye.
A long shed at the rear marked the beginning of a tunnel. The shoring was rotted and collapsing.

A bit farther west was a smaller shack with a vertical
mine shaft located in its center. There was barely room to
stand inside between the walls and the shaft. A shaky rotted
ladder extended downward beyond view. There was no
hoisting wheel mounted above the shaft, and no evidence
of one ever having been installed. Perhaps the old shaft
was used merely as an inside cooler for food storage. A horizontal tunnel penetrated the hill a few yards from the shack.

An eighth of a mile downstream was a small building
with lots of character. Some of its wide roof boards had
warped to near rain-gutter proportions. A ramshackle rear
stoop was on its last legs. The door was battened shut, but
part of the south wall was missing. I poked my head inside, and after a moment getting used to the dim light, I
made out a wooden floor and some old furniture. One step
inside was enough. With a hollow groan, the floor sagged
like a trampoline. I could make out a large trapdoor in the
center. Another shaft, no doubt. I tossed a rock onto the
trapdoor. The punky empty sound demonstrated that further exploration would be foolhardy. The solid earth outside felt reassuring. Behind this cabin were a number of
shafts nearly hidden by heavy brush. Some were covered
with three-inch-diameter poles too rotted to support one's
weight. Their partial collapse indicated that some unwary
creature had broken through.

The numerous shafts and tunnels attested to a considerable hard-rock mining effort, but it was a vain effort, for
most of the gold taken in the area was placered from Williams Creek.

In 1867, Benton Goodwin, a deaf-mute, found the first
sizeable gold deposit. He uncovered a two-dollar nugget
at the junction of Swauk and Williams creeks, when he
kicked over some rocks to make it easier to gather cooking
water. Greatly excited, he put the nugget in his mouth and
ran squawking back to camp! Members of the party panned
gold furiously all summer. Some pans ran to one thousand
dollars, and a good gravel bar yielded up to six hundred

Survivor of numerous booms and desertions, this squared log cabin is one of the more picturesque buildings on the north side of the main street in Liberty.

dollars per day. Inevitably, word leaked out, and miners poured in.

The first community established was called Meaghersville, and was located at the site of the original discovery. As gold was panned out and the hot activity moved upstream, camps were moved for convenience. The town migrated two miles up Williams Creek to its present position. By 1884 the boom had slacked, and the Chinese moved in. A few years later, white miners held mass meetings and demanded the Chinese leave. It had been determined that hydraulic operations would pay off, and deserted claims were again valuable.

Scott Darling opened a store in 1892, selling "everything you could want—Miners supplies, fishbait, gum boots, and bug juice." A post office was established and the town was officially designated "Liberty."

Liberty was nearly deserted in 1897 when the Yukon

Waters from a spring on the slope above Liberty were diverted to this wheel by an earthen ditch and wooden flume. The power generated was used to turn a drum-type gold washer.

strike lured most miners away. In 1925 a dredge was brought in from Sumpter, Oregon, and activities boomed again. Hard rockers sank shafts in search of the mother lode. Some wire gold in quartz was found, but the big lode was never tapped. During the depression, a few hard-up miners moved in to "pan wages," but pockets missed by the dredges were rare. Slowly, Liberty became deserted.

Scattered throughout town are relics typical of the various booms that Liberty enjoyed. The oldest are probably the log structures that dot both sides of the main street for nearly a quarter mile.

A number of the cabins were used for a time as places of business. Many show signs of loving care and repair. On some, the repairs are falling in disrepair. Sheets of metal roofing placed over scant shingles are loose and floppy. Thick butt shakes have been tacked over the metal and now they are falling away.

A waterwheel-powered rotary gold washer rests intact at the east edge of town. A small ditch still carries a minimal flow of water to the wooden trough that in turn feeds the water to the upper portion of the wooden wheel. The wheel stands about twelve or fourteen feet high and is equipped with perhaps four dozen slanted boards that catch the flow of water. An iron axle transports the power to a series of belts and chains which result in not only turning the drum, but in powering a small endless belt. The belt lifts the gold-bearing gravel from the bin to the mouth of the drum, where it is treated with water and agitated. Unwanted gravel flows out the far end of the drum like concrete from an overfull ready-mix truck. Periodically the drum is scoured and the gold concentrate is panned out by hand.

At the west end of town there is another gold washer. Built to more modern specifications, it operates on the same principle, but is powered by a Diesel engine, and appears to have a capacity hundreds of times that of its counterpart across town.

It was in Liberty that the "incident of the rock" supposedly occurred. A favorite story, and often repeated, it has a number of variations. . . . The grizzled old prospector, tired after ten hard hours spent on the blister end of a pick, was contentedly eating his home-cooked supper. That's when it happened! A two-ton rock came flying through the roof, smashed the table flat, and drove it, supper and all, clear

More modern counterpart to the waterwheel-powered gold washer is found "cross town," at the west end of Liberty.

through the floor. Spattered with stew, boiling mad, but unhurt, the old gentleman sat there a moment, then he rose, wiped the stew from his face, and stalked outside. He planted his feet wide and firm. With a voice heard for miles down the canyon, he bellowed, "All right, dammit—who threw it?"

An old shoemaker's establishment on the right is nearly covered by underbrush. The buildings on the left are obviously newer and not a part of the original Blewett.

BLEWETT, WASHINGTON

There are a number of historical accounts concerning the town of Blewett. I read two of them and found little agreement. A third account sided with neither of the first two, hence the vague nature of the following few items, chosen because they were consistent in some small measure.

Gold in quartz or nugget form was found by a soldier, perhaps a captain, in 1854 or 1855. The town started about 1861. The area was noted either for its small nuggets found only near bedrock, or its thousand-dollar nuggets found nearly everywhere.

About 1874, gold in quartz was found in nearby Culver Gulch. The veins ran narrow and rich, or up to eight feet wide. In 1880, the action slowed and the town died—or— the place was a boomer until 1890, when the rush was in full swing! A twenty-stamp mill was built in 1879 by the Chelan Mining Co. For a while it turned out ten thousand gold bricks a week.

Some of the facts are obviously "Chamber of Commerce." Like the ten thousand bricks a week. Any gold brick worth its name weighs at least thirty pounds and was worth, in 1890, about ten thousand dollars. Now ten thousand bricks a week adds up to one hundred million dollars in gold per week—far more than the area's lifetime production.

Blewett's past is hidden behind a disastrous fire, and the destruction of most of the surviving buildings by construc-

Twenty stamps once crushed ore supplied by the many tunnels located nearby. Culver Gulch, to the right a bit and behind the mill, had more than a dozen tunnels in its first mile.

tion of a highway through town. Later the highway was made wider, and Blewett's visible trace of history became even narrower.

About all one can be sure of in Blewett is that the site is located twenty-one miles north of Liberty, and if you don't look close, you will miss it.

Four buildings remain on the north side of the road, two of them original structures of Blewett. One is said to have been a shoemaker's establishment, the other a woodshed.

One of the finest arrastras in existence today. Approximately six feet in diameter and deeply grooved, it is complete with two of its "drag rocks." Rainwater stands in the groove once occupied by gold ore. Ground to sandlike consistency by the orbiting crushers, the gold was then recovered by hand panning.

Across the highway are two structures of more obvious background. One, an old stamp mill, shows that four bays of stamps were once in action. A bay of stamps was traditionally five stamps. Near the mill is the old smithy, with a few items of original gear still within.

What makes a visit to Blewett worthwhile is the marvelous old stone arrastra. This drag-stone ore crusher, built in 1861 or 1874, is said to have been waterpower driven. The explanation seems likely, since it is located adjacent to Peshastin Creek. Much of the ore from the earlier shafts and tunnels was processed here for a percentage of the gold retrieved.

Dozens of prospect holes and horizontal tunnels can be found within a mile or so of Blewett. According to the *Liberty, Washington, 15 minute topographic map*, more than a dozen tunnels are located in Culver Gulch immediately behind the old mill.

*Weathered and warped, these look-alike homes have seen occupancy
by loggers of both the horse and gasoline eras.*

DISAUTEL, WASHINGTON

Disautel stands alone, far removed from the other ghost
towns visited in the state of Washington. It is not shown
on the area map at the beginning of the chapter, but may be
located on the *Disautel, Washington, 15 minute topographic
map*. From Omak, in north-central Washington, gravel road
155 heads east. In fifteen miles, a lesser road branches to
the right (south), crosses Omak Creek, and immediately
branches into the various streets of Disautel.

*An old structure at the edge of Disautel, the last remnant of a
dismantled house. Only the rear wall and washhouse remain.*

To the left is a huge garage, and beyond are a number of
residences, one of them occupied. The road to the right leads
past a row of look-alike homes, then winds by a number of
residences of mixed vintage. On the hill is a strange-looking
structure. It appears to be a small store with a gabled
false front complete with a pointless window that opens to
the air in both directions.

Louis Whistocken, who lives in town, was happy to talk

In Disautel the kids and ponies swim together. Headlong gallops and diving dismounts make the old swimming hole a lively training ground for future bronc busters.

The "Brooks Place," at the north edge of Disautel, has long been deserted. Young boys living across the creek are positive the house is haunted.

about the history of Disautel, and discuss the nature of its remnants.

The funny structure on the hill was not a store, but the rear wall and washhouse of a home that had been partially dismantled. The large building in the center of town was once a barn for logging teams, then a garage for logging trucks. Louis explained that the trucks put many of the loggers out of work. A railroad once carried logs from Disautel to the sawmill at Omak. When the area was logged out, the Highway Department used the garage for housing road maintaining equipment. Later, when the Highway Department moved out, the town died. Only two families remained.

Louis Whistocken is a handsome man of Indian ancestry. His last name was his dad's first name, and meant "walk on the arm." Louis hastened to add that his father, in spite of his name, was a very well-educated man. Louis' main interest was rodeo, until he got bent up. "Busted my knees a few times—had three specialties, steer ropin', bull doggin' and saddle bronc. Used to win my share of prize money— even after my knees gave out."

On the way out of town I came upon two more bronc busters. The meeting was a near collision. It looked like I would head them off at the bridge but at the last moment the two young riders veered their mounts sharply and headed for the stream. At full speed, they flew over the backs of their ponies and splashed heavily in the water. Shortly, they both emerged, laughing—each hanging onto his pony's tail, enjoying a tail drag onto dry land. Remounted, they galloped off, then turned and headed back to repeat their performance. I stopped the truck and stepped out, camera in hand. The encore was outstanding. The third go-round was even better, and the fourth performance rated a cold bottle of pop all around.

We sat on the tailgate of my truck and talked. Dave was twelve and Leon was fourteen. They were brothers, sharing the last name of St. Peter. Their father had been killed riding saddle bronc at a rodeo a few years back. In spite of this, the two boys both plan to become championship rodeo hands.

Dave pointed out the old Brooks residence just across the creek. It was "the ghostiest place around."

Leon chimed in, "We stayed over there once—clear after it got dark—scared us—it sure is haunted!"

I looked back as I drove away. I could see the two of them shaking up the last of their pop—then thumbing the stream of foam carefully against their tongues—and each other.

WASHINGTON AREA 2

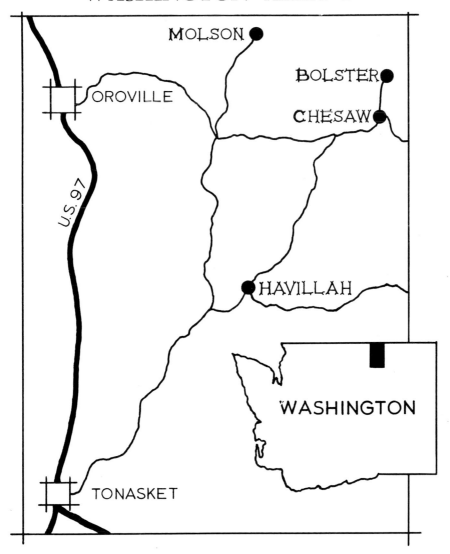

MOLSON, WASHINGTON

THE WOODED SLOPES and fractured ridges that make up the
Okanogan Highlands in north-central Washington consti-
tute a ghost town hunter's paradise. Here, within a few
miles of the Canadian border, are the remains of four ghost
towns. Born of a short-lived mining boom, they maintained

a shaky existence through the early 1900's as agricultural communities.

The last to die was Molson, or more correctly, the three Molsons. The story is unbelievable, but thoroughly documented.

John Molson, investor, and George Meacham, promoter, decided to combine their respective funds and talents to create a town. Molson, the man with the money, had large sums invested in the Poland China Gold Mine. The mine was located high on the North Fork of Mary Ann Creek, just two miles south of the Canadian border, and not considered a fit site for the town. A flat area four miles west of the mine was selected, and the town laid out. Named for Molson, but never graced by his presence, the town grew from nothing in 1900 to a population of three hundred in one year. Then the town nearly died when Meacham, the promoter, had a bad hassle with the new town fathers and left for Texas.

In the first year the promoters had invested seventy-five thousand dollars. A drugstore was built, and a dentist and a lawyer set up practice. The Molson Magnate was to have printed up the first paper. Perhaps a few issues were run off the presses, but no one recalls ever having seen a copy.

The ornate three-story Tonasket Hotel was the big drawing card. It had a full-glass front, and a wrap-around second-story ballustrade. More than sixty full-height windows gave the three-story structure an impressive appearance. The two outboard windows on the false front were strictly decoration. They smacked of empty promotion, as did brochures showing steamboats coming up Baker River to dock near the hotel. Baker Creek was in reality the seepage of a few springs a mile to the south.

Ore deposits at the Poland China were thinning and Molson suffered. For several years the town seemed to be doomed. Then a trickle of homesteaders appeared. In 1904, W. W. Parry built a store and grain warehouse. Rumors of a railroad were widely spread in 1905, and a new mercantile went into business. The railroad crews did, in fact, build the tracks right past town. Eight saloons grew from the ground overnight "like mushrooms," and a deputy was hired. The town was booming and lots were selling at a premium. Then J. H. McDonald filed his homestead. No one had bothered about land ownership, and old McDonald had a farm of considerable wealth after he planted the

The bank of "Old Molson" was originally built on skids in the middle of the street, then moved about town, doing business while searching for a legal lot on which to land.

corners of his legally allotted one hundred and sixty acres. His quarter section of land included forty acres of Molson, Hotel Tonasket included!

Legal notices to vacate were posted, and lawsuits led to countersuits. Storekeeper Parry considered the situation hopeless, and built a new mercantile half a mile north. Several businesses followed, and a new residential area was created. Lots in the new Molson had the advantage of uncontested ownership. By 1906, New Molson and Old Molson were of equal size and temperament.

Arguments never stopped, and fistfights were common occurrences. A gun fight was threatened once when a resident named Sutherland complained of his neighbor's pigs trespassing on his property. Sutherland met his adversary in the middle of Main Street, with two loaded .45's. He offered one to his opponent, but was refused. The fight was a failure, but the pig problem was permanently resolved.

By 1908, McDonald had fenced in the old town of Molson. That year, Mr. L. L. Work decided to build a bank. He chose Old Molson, but could not gain legal ownership of a suitable plot of ground, so the bank was built on skids in the middle of Main Street. It opened for business a different place each morning. Finally a lot was designated and the bank was ceremoniously planted. Procedures were temporarily interrupted when the participants paused to watch, then take part in one of the better street fights in Molson's history.

Miraculously, in 1914 the two enemy camps combined efforts "for the good of our kids," and built a three-story brick schoolhouse. It had a gymnasium in the basement, and steam heat in every room, but the two outhouses were still placed out back as a sanitary measure.

Built precisely halfway between the two towns, the school became the nucleus of a third town. Those tired of fighting in the name of town pride were quick to build homes and places of business in "Center Molson." Potter built a mercantile, and Dunn built a fancy theater. Addition of a barbershop and pool hall made the new "town" the entertainment spa of the surrounding territory.

The two extremes of Molson continued to fight. If one had a new dance hall, the other built one. When an auto dealer began to sell Oaklands in Old Molson, a dealership was quickly established in New Molson selling Maxwells. Proud owners drove to Center Molson to compare notes. Old Mol-

The three-story school of Center Molson was the result of the only cooperative effort undertaken by the quarreling factions of New and Old Molson.

son had the post office, so New Molson campaigned to have one of their citizens elected postmaster. They succeeded in 1920, but Old Molson wouldn't give up the post office. When the old postmaster went to lunch, a few New Molsonites stole the works and moved it to "its rightful location."

The fights and arguments continued into the twenties, but they were largely academic, since all three towns were shrinking due to improved transportation and the removal of the railroad. As often happens when business fails, the hotels and stores burned down one by one. A few of the stores struggled on for a number of years. One of them lasted until 1955.

S. E. DIAMOND
GEN. MDSE.
RPM MOTOR OIL

STORE FOR SALE INQUIRE WITHIN OR....

*. . . or what?
Unfinished sign offers
a good buy. The
store is on the main
intersection of New
Molson and contains
some of its original
only slightly fire-
damaged merchandise.*

*New Molson had the
headquarters building
of the Eastern
Okanogan Telephone
Company. Note the
well-worn broom at
the corner of the porch
and the old main-
street buildings in the
background.*

The railroad tracks have been removed, but access to the various Molsons is still easy. The road east from Oroville is a good blacktopped secondary. Fifteen miles out, a gravel road branches to the left. About six miles north on this road stand the remains of the three Molsons. The *Mount Bonaparte, Washington, 15 minute map* shows the layout of the Molsons as well as Chesaw, Bolster, and Havillah.

Now, in 1970, all of the stores in the three Molsons are closed and the school is deserted. Only a handful of people are left to carry on the fight, and they seem to be uninterested.

At Old Molson, three buildings have been preserved. Among them is the old bank building. Fully equipped with memorabilia of the times, it is an excellent museum of the early 1900 agricultural era. Surrounding the old bank is a multitude of ancient farm machinery. Horsepowered saws, steampowered tractors, threshers, reapers, and cultivators are there.

At New Molson, or just plain Molson, a T-shaped intersection is lined with nearly a dozen substantial buildings. Outstanding are the Pratt and Chamberlin two-story rock or concrete structures that were built in 1913. On the corner is the C. L. Diamond Store with a sign in front stating "For Sale, inquire within or. . . ." And that is all. Fire has destroyed part of the interior, but much of the counterwork and some scattered merchandise are still inside. Next to the Diamond Store is a wood and metal building that is still full of old hardware. Nails, rusty bolts, bent gutter work and other worthless items are strewn all about. The sign on the front reads "McCoys Cash Store—Meats and Groceries."

A hundred yards south of the Diamond Store is the quaint old broad-porched headquarters building of the Eastern Okanogan Telephone Company. Its picturesque multi-paned front window and pompous false front make it the classic structure of Molson.

Center Molson has the school and grange hall. The school has a TV antenna on its roof, and cord after cord of weathered firewood stacked at its foundation. The basketball court is still in the school basement. It isn't hard to imagine a game in progress, Bitter enemies must have gathered here to sit in close proximity. Perhaps they even joined together momentarily to give three cheers for the Molson basketball team.

Minnie Carpenter's "Home Millinery" was one of three hat shops in town. The building later became the town's funeral parlor, and even later a garage for Model T's.

CHESAW, WASHINGTON

Ten miles east of the Molson Junction, on the banks of Meyers Creek, stands the town of Chesaw. Once the prime rival of the Molsons, it has been reduced by time and fire to a precious few buildings. A country store continues in operation and a dozen or so people live nearby. Once a year, on the Fourth of July, up to six thousand people flock to the famous Chesaw Fair and Rodeo, and Chesaw looks like its old self again—but on this quiet summer day, only one car was parked on Main Street.

Beyond the little general store is a small log structure that has been converted to a double-doored garage. In 1900, this was Minnie Carpenter's "Home Millinery" shop. In its display windows the latest feathered fashions were changed as rapidly as styles required. There were several other hat shops, among them "Mrs. Commodore Johnson's Millinery Shop," where the tastes of the younger generation were courted.

The bank building of Chesaw had an extra-fancy false front. The "Townsite Building" is in the background, its false front proclaiming an elegance not evident inside.

North of Minnie's Millinery is the false-fronted Townsite Building. Once there was a bold sign along its flank reading "TOWNSITE OFFICE" indicating it was a real-estate office, or town hall; perhaps both. Between the Townsite Building and Minnie's is the largest remaining building in Chesaw. It has been used for a number of purposes, but is best remembered as the Chesaw Bank. Later it was the town's post office, and more recently it has served as a residence.

J. P. Blaine's assay office at the northern edge of Chesaw still has its original partitions and work benches. The building was erected in 1898, and was the first assay office in the county.

One of the first mining services offered in Chesaw was that of assayer, J. P. Blaine. His small smelter and laboratory building stands on the right side of the street at the extreme north end of town. The hipped-roof, square-log structure is plumb and sound of wall, but its shingles are blowing away in batches, and the lean-to shed behind is in a shambles. The tree that stands behind matches the building, with sturdy trunk topped with broken limbs and dead branches.

A quarter mile north of town are the squat remains of a two-story log and frame house. Once a beautiful home, it now presents a study in angularity. The left gable leans

This artistically collapsed home a quarter of a mile north of Chesaw is of undetermined origin but of unmatched angularity.

out. The ridgepole has broken and permitted the roof to drop at the center. One corner has sunk and carried one side of the entry cubicle with it, creating another set of distortions from the vertical.

Chesaw was named after "Chee-Saw," an early Chinese settler who took an Indian wife and settled near a commonly traveled ford on Meyers Creek. In the 1800's visitors to Chee-Saw's Ford spotted some traces of gold in the creek. Word of the gold spread, but since the area was in the Colville Indian Reservation, no prospecting was allowed. In 1896, with morals adjusted to fit the pocketbook, the white man opened half the reservation to mineral claims. Promptly, most of the good pastures and fields were taken by whites as placer claims. The townsite of Chesaw was laid out on land obtained by filing a half-dozen false claims side by side. Some honest mineral claims were made, however, on outcrops that looked promising. Iron and copper were the first ores taken in hard-rock operations. Considerable iron has come from the Aster, Polaris, and the Roosevelt. The placer gold was "spotty." One claim might yield eighty dollars a pan, and twenty feet away another claim would be worthless.

The Gold Axe on Buckhorn Mountain was the first to produce gold from hard rock. Eventually high-grade ore was produced in quantity, and mills were built at the north edge of Chesaw and at a road junction about three miles to the south.

By 1900 Chesaw was a sizeable log community of two hundred population. It grew rapidly into a full-blown town with two three-story frame hotels, and a population (on a Saturday night, and counting dogs) that neared the one-thousand mark.

Josh Clary's "Greenwood" was the busiest saloon in town. Fred Fine's paper, the *Meyers Creek News,* aligned itself solidly with the editorial policies of the Republican party, and printed a little news on the side.

The Barker Hotel burned in 1906, and two years later three more of the town's larger buildings were destroyed. Mining operations were dropping off as lodes were depleted. The Greenwood Saloon was sold and converted to a church. A steeple was tacked on the roof, extending only slightly above the saloon's false front.

In the twenties, the automobile led people to the bigger towns, and Chesaw declined at an increasing rate. Many buildings were scavenged. Fire racked the town in 1950 and again in 1959.

But the population of Chesaw is now increasing. Recently a couple bought the old eight-sided silo behind the general store. Stained a dark brown and fitted with a spiral staircase and handsome front door, it makes a proper summer home.

A saloon building with a halfhearted false front and pretentious windows. The building to the right, probably a store, was unfancied and nearly windowless.

BOLSTER, WASHINGTON

D. C. Jenkins was the editor of the *Bolster Drill.* Generally outspoken, he was particularly acidic as he wrote his last editorial. He had learned why so few subscriptions had been bought. Most readers borrowed the paper. Some even split the cost and passed the paper around. Editor Jenkins wrote: "To those upon whose backs a fungus growth sere and yellow is clinging. . . . Those who for the past year have borrowed the paper . . . which wasn't no good no how, I offer my sympathy!" He closed his office and left town.

Bolster, just two miles north of Chesaw, once threatened to outshine its southern rival. For one year, each called the other a "suburb."

It was in 1899 that J. S. McBride bought up the Commonwealth Placer Claim, paced off a main street, named the

This low-cut log structure was last occupied by one of seven bachelor prospectors, the final residents of Bolster. The old saloon and store are in the background.

place "Bolster," and proceeded to sell lots. The Hamilton Store was already there, and soon a corner of the store was designated as post office, with the storekeeper as postmaster. Within a year, two more stores sprang into action, and three saloons opened up. Thirty homes were built, and Editor Jenkins started up the paper with high hopes of success. A three-story hotel, the mark of success in these parts, was constructed, but never quite finished.

Bolster collapsed! It seemed to follow the mining trend closer than Chesaw, and perhaps the loss of its newspaper had some effect. The town's people drifted to Chesaw and Molson. The post office closed in 1909. School opened for one year in 1910, then closed. By 1916 the only citizens left were seven bachelor prospectors, and they finally left or died.

*Havillah's second Lutheran church, built in 1917, still offers services in
spite of a shaky footbridge. The ladies' "powder room"
is out back, first building on the left.*

The remains are sparse. A large false-fronted saloon stands at the edge of a cultivated field. Its three bay windows are vacant. A false front extends half-heartedly toward the ridgepole, and part of it is blown away. The north wall sags and will soon fall, and will probably take the rest of the building with it. Just beyond the saloon is a similar structure, but without a false front. It may have been a store, but has been used as a barn so long that all signs of human occupancy are gone. Half a dozen cabins are scattered about, last used, perhaps, by the seven lonely prospectors.

There isn't much left to see or explore at Bolster. The few old buildings seem sad and dejected. Only one man could look upon this lonely scene with any measure of satisfaction. That man would be Editor Jenkins.

HAVILLAH, WASHINGTON

In 1903, Martin Schweikert built a gristmill and store near the junction of Antoine Creek and Mill Creek, at a point three miles west and ten miles southwest by road from Chesaw. Business was good; in a few years Mr. Schweikert, the town's first postmaster, built a larger steam-powered flour mill. The boiler and other parts were railroaded into Molson, and then freighted sixteen miles to Havillah by oxen. Grain storage buildings were constructed, and soon fine white flour was flowing from the mill. Packed in carefully weighed sacks, it sold far and wide under the trade name of "Gold Sheaf."

Soon a log school was built, and a Lutheran church constructed. Havillah, pronounced "HaVEElah," was rapidly approaching its maximum size.

In 1917 a handsome new tall-spired church was built. A deep ravine cuts across in front of the church, requiring access via a wooden footbridge. Although the bridge is in doubtful repair, and the church looks somewhat tattered at the windows, the sign out front proclaims weekly services led by Reverend Winterstein.

The little log schoolhouse has become an outbuilding for one of the remaining residents. Stoutly resisting decay, with windows boarded over, it is hung all about with the wire, ladders, cables, chains and the miscellaneous parts that farmers always save.

Havillah's original schoolhouse was plain and stout. Built about 1902, it has survived well and now does duty as a farm outbuilding.

Havillah's old steampowered flour mill was converted to Havillah's second school. A fancy wrap-around stairway satisfied the fire code.

When the Schweikert mill closed down, it was converted to a school. A second-story access had to be added as a fire escape. Enclosed, and lighted by two small windows, the stairway cranks its way down the side of the building, around the corner, and ends at the next corner, having traversed nearly half of the building's perimeter.

Havillah isn't much of a place anymore, of course. It never did measure out to be much of a place—until you added up the friendships, the memories, and the good times that were yesterday in Havillah.

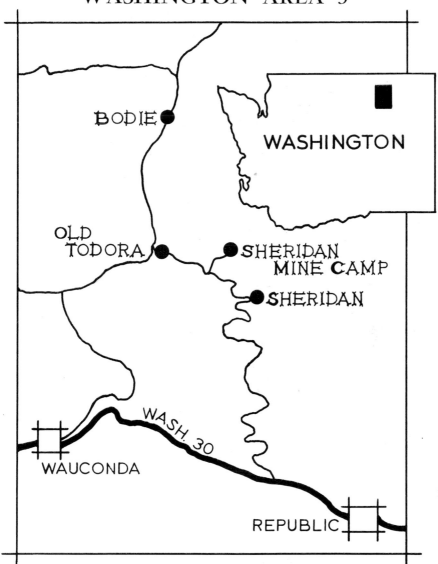

BODIE, WASHINGTON

THE ROAD NORTHEAST from Wauconda parallels Todora
Creek along its entire length, terminating at the creek's
juncture with Kettle River. About midway along this scenic
route, fifteen miles from Wauconda, is the site of Bodie,

*The cabin in the foreground has been freshly chinked but is in need of
new tar paper on its gable. The second cabin displays a
sign reading: "Survivors will be prosecuted."*

Washington. Forested slopes broken by occasional barren
outcrops and footed by grassy flats make the trip to Bodie
one of pleasant variation. Todora Creek bounces along,
nearly always visible from the road, and gently audible at
each crossing. The *Bodie Mountain, Washington, 15 minute
topografhic map* is a definite aid to exploration. Part of this
map is reproduced in the Introduction.

Bodie has half a dozen buildings strung out along the road,
mostly on the east side, next to the creek. Most of the cabins
are stained board and batten. Only one is of log construction. Across the street is the deserted Bodie school, complete with woodshed and twin houses out back. The second
story of the schoolhouse appears to have been an apartment,
perhaps an early version of a teacherage.

Bodie was established as a mill town about 1900. At one
time it had a store, post office, cookhouse, bunkhouse, and
hotel. Almost every resident worked for the Perkins Milling Company. The giant stamp mill processed much of the

Bleached boards and white clouds reflect the slanted light of the moon, adding to the ghostly quality of Bodie.

*Bodie School remained active long after
the town had lost its post office.*

ore taken from the Golden Reward and the Elk (later the
Golconda) mines. Business was good up until the late thirties. The mill shut down—and so did Bodie. In 1962 the mill
burned. Since then, things have been pretty quiet.

You can almost hear the silence in Bodie, especially at sun-
set. Later, by moonlight, the old cabins in town take on a
new look. Bleached boards seem luminous, and fence posts
show half outlines. Clouds scattered above reflect the dim
light and stand out boldly against the pitch-dark sky.

The morning light divorced Bodie of its nocturnal beauty. Some of the cabins looked downright dingy. One, however, was in fine trim, recently repaired, and protected by
a sign that made me think twice:

"NO TRESPASSING—SURVIVORS WILL BE PROSE-
CUTED."

OLD TORODA, WASHINGTON

Indian trails generally followed the streams, and the white man often built his wagon roads on top of the trails. Consequently, where streams joined, roads also met, and there towns sprang into being.

Toroda was established at the confluence of Cougar and Toroda creeks, northeast of Wauconda. It mushroomed into existence shortly after 1896 when the area was opened to mineral claims. By 1898 there were twenty-five cabins strung out along the intersection. Aligned on both sides of the north-south road, there were a store, smithy, assay office, and post office.

It appeared to be a growing town, but rumors concerning the nearby mines were circulating shortly after its post office was established. The suggestion was made to move the town north four miles where the mines were more promising. The town stayed, of course, but eight months after Toroda received its post office, it was moved and given the

The assay office is no longer in business, due to a lack of ore samples and a bad leak in the roof.

The dilapidated smithy is in the foreground, with the Schmeling General Store beyond. The overhang on the store front was designed to attract customers to its shade and, hopefully, to draw them inside to make purchases.

name of Bodie. Later a post office opened twenty miles farther northeast, using the name Toroda. The original Toroda then took on its present designation, "Old Toroda."

Along Old Toroda's main street are three of its original business houses and a number of cabins. One of the cabins on the east side of the main street was probably the residence and office of Postmaster Frederick Rosenfelt. Just north is the badly decayed structure that once housed the local assayer's office. Its walls are sagging and its roof poles are nearly barren of shingles. On the west side of the street the blacksmith's shop stands nearly roofless. Its solid log walls are well joined, and its gables enclosed with broad rough-hewn boards. Adjacent and to the north, is the Schmeling General Store, once operated by brothers, Carl and Herman. The roof was extended six feet to the front to provide shade for window-shoppers and inveterate whittlers.

Just west of Old Toroda is a modern country home. I stopped in to ask about Old Toroda, and was heartily welcomed by the Atchisons. Over huge stacks of pancakes topped with buttered syrup, we discussed the deserted towns and mining camps in the area. After determining the nature of each building in Old Toroda, I mentioned that my *Bodie Mountain, Washington, Topographic (15 minute)* map indicated a large mine three miles upstream on Cougar Creek. The Atchison brothers, S. G. and Charlie, confirmed its existence and elaborated. Called the Sheridan Mine Camp, it had a number of buildings including a mill and dormitory. That made it a ghost town in my book. I thanked the Atchisons and headed for the door. Before I could leave, Charlie added, "You might go on up a couple of miles and look over the old town of Sheridan. There's a dozen buildings there, some made of logs—three stories high —and a hotel with dance hall on the second floor—balcony, too!"

The map was quickly spread and the site located. Beside the first sharp switchback above the head of the creek were two empty squares, indicating deserted buildings. Charlie was surprised the map showed even that much. "It's on the old Sheridan Road, you know—used to go all the way to Republic, but it's been blocked with trees for years."

Mrs. Atchison volunteered, "Not too many people know about the place—last bunch in there punctured their oil pan. We had to go up and rescue their car. Of course they had to walk all the way down."

Amidst warnings of deep ruts and boulder-strewn switchbacks, I thanked them for pancakes and information, then set off for Sheridan Camp and Sheridan Town.

*The building in the left foreground is probably a dining-room—
bunkhouse combination. The small structure behind
is either a cookshack or a meat house.*

SHERIDAN MINE CAMP, WASHINGTON

The road was exactly as stated—terrible. Ruts were a
foot deep. The first three-fourths of a mile was bad, but
after making the left turn to go up the East Fork of Cougar
Creek, the road became a challenge. Heavy trucks had been
through here when the ground was wet and soft. Narrow
ridges between ruts were now the roadway, and accurate
navigation was a must. In two miles, a gate blocked the
road, but here was the turnoff heading left up to the mine
camp. A sort of halfway house was located at the junction.
It was a handsome cabin of large logs, roofed with moss-
grown thick-butt cedar shingles.

Half a mile north of the halfway house junction was the
Sheridan Camp cookhouse and bunkhouse. Eleven logs high,
and steeply roofed, it offered room for cooking, heating, and
recreation, with sleeping quarters above. Behind the bunkhouse was a board and batten shed with an air-circulating
cupola on top. I speculated that it was either a meat house
or assay office, or perhaps the cooking was done here instead of in the big log building. One of the nice features
of exploring an "unknown" site is that the only information
available is "on the spot" guesswork. One thing was certain.

Heavy timbers of a "mill-like" building show little of the expected brace work that would hold heavy stamp machinery.

The twelve-by-eighteen-foot vented building had been built around a four-foot-diameter stump, sawed flat at table height and full of chop marks! That meant it most likely had been a meat house or cookhouse. The assay office theory was ruled out.

There was little room for the buildings at the mine camp. The structure clinging to the hillside was either a small mill, a concentrator, or a large ore loader.

Just up the hill a bit of the old mill clings to the hillside, extending down to and including half the roadway. In fact, the road splits to go either past or under the mill chutes. The mill is in bad shape. Much of its superstructure is gone, and its ironwork and machinery are missing. Perhaps I shouldn't call it a mill, for its inside timbering did not resemble most mills. It could have been a concentrator, or merely a fancy loader. Near the "mill" was a square two-story building. Some of the original equipment was inside, and the function of this structure was evident. Forge tables, with cinders and charcoal still in place, made it a smithy. Numerous ore samples littered one end of the building. In a small, closed portion, there was an abundance of crushed ore. An oven pedestal and roof vent were enough to deduce that an assayer carried out his work at this end of the building.

The road was narrow, and it took a while to find a place wide enough to turn about. For a time I suspected that I had driven in on the ultimate one-way road—"in only." Finally, a one-eighty accomplished, I headed for Sheridan Town with high expections.

Massive and windowless, the two-and-a-half-story log "hotel"
of Sheridan was probably never occupied.

SHERIDAN, WASHINGTON

From the "halfway house" the road leads through an unlocked gate, and continues upstream along the north bank of the East Fork of Cougar Creek. The roadway is narrow. There is no flat area on either side of the "straight" road for a mile and a half. The first turn is a sharp switchback to the right. At this point a faint roadway leads straight ahead. The barely perceptible track was the main street of Sheridan.

Looming on the right, and fairly hidden by trees, was a two-and-a-half-story "hotel." Each story was eight logs high, and the logs were fat—well over a foot in diameter. It was another eight logs to the gable top. Twenty-four logs high and still standing! Across the front of the lower floor was a long timbered opening designed to hold two double doors and several large windows. The lower foundation logs extended forward a dozen feet to support a wide boardwalk, now entirely rotted away. Close inspection indicated that company offices may have been planned for the main floor, with living quarters above.

Just up the main road a few yards was another log building of nearly equal size. It looked like another "hotel," but more probably was built to house the laboring force.

A close-up view of the window frames and door jambs of the big log building reveals no evidence of window sash or door hinge. Apparently the town died with one of its largest buildings only half completed.

Centered, and behind these two massive log buildings was a third log structure. It was a low, single-story outfit, with collapsed roof. Numerous low walls divided it into stalls, spelling out its function. It was a stable, and it was a big one—larger in floor space than either of the taller log buildings.

The faint trail that led into the trees from the switchback became more indistinct with every step. I had gone perhaps one hundred yards beyond the two-and-a-half-story log "hotel" when I came across the collapsed remains of the real *hotel*!

It had been gigantic—and plush. Squared logs formed

Deluxe hand-squared log walls supported an expensive tongue-and-groove dance floor on the story above. Dancing was the favorite form of entertainment in Sheridan.

tall, single-story side walls. Adz marks on the logs indicated they had been flattened without the benefit of saws. The corners were beautifully lock-jointed. Above the first floor had been a vaulted peaked roof, constructed of sawed rafters and shingled with heavy shakes. The entire upper floor—clear out to the useless eaves—was floored smooth with expensive (for that era) tongue and groove boards.

This was the fancy place the Atchison brothers at Old Todora had told me about. It had been intact just a few years before. The upper floor was used for dances, and had a walk-out veranda. Below the veranda was the usual boardwalk leading into the lower floor, which was the hotel proper.

The rest of the town was anticlimactic. Behind the hotel was a large dug-out cooler. West and north of the hotel were six cabins in various states of decay. One of them had roof

One of six small cabins standing along the barely visible streets of Sheridan. The building is in remarkably good condition for its age—seventy-five years.

shakes nearly three feet long, and everything was so well preserved that it could have been made liveable with a few hours' labor.

Never had I been in a more deserted or more forgotten town, nor had I ever seen such magnificent log buildings. Just how they had survived was a mystery. The big log building at the switchback was a mystery by itself. Something was "wrong" with its appearance. It took a moment —then it was obvious. There were no windows at the sides or on the upper floors. No sane man would live in a flammable building without an avenue of escape. A building like this had to have windows. At first it seemed unexplainable. Then things began to add up. Old Toroda, a few miles downstream, had held its post office for only eight months. The reason was that the mines nearby were failing. Could it be that Sheridan failed just as quickly, and that work on the big log building was stopped short, just before the windows were slated to be cut out and framed?

Perhaps the reasoning is in error. In a way, I hope it is, for standing in the middle of this impressive ghost town, one begins to feel guilty about prying into long-held secrets.

Like a grand old lady, Sheridan town deserves her modicum of privacy.

PART III
IDAHO

IDAHO AREA 1

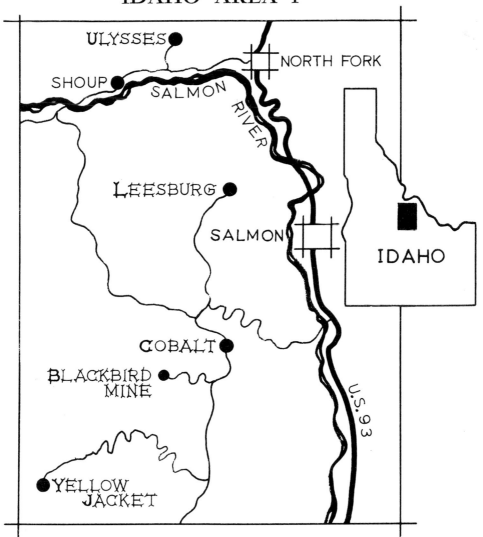

LEESBURG, IDAHO

THE HIGH COUNTRY of Idaho is endowed with nature's fullest measure. Tall mountains, big trees, rushing waters, and deep blue skies are combined in beautiful proportion. But beauty is seldom found without a touch of adversity.

Of adversities, logging trucks and narrow roads are two

The once busy street of Leesburg was built wide enough to tie "team and rig" on both sides and still have room for two-way traffic.

of Idaho's most challenging. The two hazards are invariably encountered together. Although roads are of noted solidarity, they appear to be thoroughly flexible when viewed through this observer's phobia. The road shrinks to fractional width whenever a logging truck approaches. The narrow portion of the road seemingly travels ahead of the vehicle, accompanied by a shock wave of fear and despair. Even the boldest seek shelter, or lacking that will huddle precariously at road's edge.

I had been in Idaho for less than an hour when a logging truck put me in the ditch. It was on the well-traveled Salmon River Road, north of Salmon and west of North Fork. The logger insisted on the middle of the road. That gave me an option on the ditch, which I quickly assumed. Later I learned that a logger had dropped his rig into the river a

*The heavy snows of a hundred winters have finally broken the
back of this proud structure. The triple ridgepoles
served only to postpone its fate.*

few days earlier. The driver had been over-courteous, and
his right wheels, too close to the edge, broke down the fill
at the river's edge. The truck flipped and rolled into the
white waters of the Salmon River. Other drivers quite naturally decided thereafter to use the center half of the road.

One of the foresters at the Indianola Ranger Station indicated that I was not the only victim. A number of tourists
had reported similar encounters. The ranger advised,
"Just pull over, close your eyes, and think thin." He also
advised that the back road into Leesburg was presently used
by loggers. I decided to take a longer but more relaxing
route.

Leesburg* is reached most pleasantly by going south of
the town of Salmon for about five miles on U.S. Highway 93,

---

*See Cobalt, Idaho, for map information.

then turning west on the Williams Creek Road. Fourteen miles up this steep, all-weather road is Williams Creek Summit. Beyond the summit, the road parallels Moccasin Creek, reaching downstream eight miles to its junction with Napias Creek. A right turn here leads you seven hard miles up Napias Creek to Leesburg. The road is narrow and rocky, changing to a badly rutted dirt surface for the last few miles. Just past the crossing of Camp Creek, the road angles to the right and enters a large grassy meadow. The main street—two ruts with grass between—stretches eastward across the flat, flanked on the north by perhaps a dozen log structures. Fewer but more impressive buildings line the south side of the road. Ahead, the aspens close the road to a narrow path, and dark green pines stretch up the slope, topping out at the skyline.

The first building on the north side is a small, low, double-walled log cabin, probably used as a cooler or powder house. Toward the middle of town is a long, extensively sway-backed log store, its low, wide walls bulging and bending as the collapsing roof spends its weight. Nearby a ridgepole slants nakedly, the few remaining roof boards clinging momentarily. Across the street, a low-ceilinged two-story log store stands roofless and in near ruin, its gable end leaning as if nodding in sleep. Two of the cabins along the overgrown street are occupied.

Although often told, the story of Leesburg can withstand yet another try, especially in the light of some "new" information uncovered at the Lemhi Museum in Salmon.

Prospectors in northern Montana had heard the rumor of a stream of gold high up in the southwest hills. Five miners, following directions given them by friendly Indians, worked their way up the Nez Perce Trail, over the divide, across several drainages, to the high slopes overlooking the present site of Leesburg. The sediments of the many tributary streams were panned, and on August 12, 1866, gold-rich gravels were found. The five miners named the stream "Napias," after the Indian word for gold.

Word leaked out, and by summer's end three thousand miners had filed as many claims along seven miles of stream. A town sprang up, named for General Robert E. Lee, populated mainly by Southerners. Not to be outdone, the Northerners established Grantsville, about a half mile upstream on Napias Creek. Grantsville has been erroneously located one mile west of Leesburg, placing it high on a timbered

The last remaining two-story building at Leesburg is complete
with doorways at both levels. Low ceilings minimized
the winter heating problem.

hillside, an unlikely home for gold-hungry placer miners.
The two towns soon grew into one, and the entire town went
by the name favored by the majority. In 1870 there were
more than one hundred businesses located on the main street
of Leesburg. Most of the stores had dirt floors. A few of the
finer establishments sported cowhide carpets.

By 1874 the town was nearly deserted and the Chinese
moved in to scour the sands for riches overlooked. Five
years later, the Chinese were massacred. The total number
killed is not known, but one survived to report the tragic
event. The Indians were blamed, but later evidence indicated it may have been the work of an outlaw gang.

The gold was gone by 1940. Even the last-ditch hy-
draulickers had given up. Sixteen million dollars' worth of
gold had been panned and sluiced from the gravel bars of

Shingles were rare in Leesburg. Most buildings had board-and-batten roofs, which leaked reliably at the lightest drizzle.

Napias Creek. The population soon dropped to less than one hundred. In 1944 it fell to two, then dropped from two to zero.

In 1969 (Leesburg's centennial year) two young bearded men chose to reoccupy the long-deserted town. Squatter's rights seem adequate, and their quasi-legal status bothers them little. They look and act as if they belong in Leesburg, and their presence is a beneficial deterrent to the erosionary effects of eager souvenir hunters.

Strictly a company town, the buildings of Cobalt are of similar construction with aluminum roofs, white asbestos siding, and green trim.

COBALT (BLACKBIRD), IDAHO

"Do not fail to visit Cobalt. It isn't very old, but it sure is dead." The same advice came from a number of people in Salmon. Notable among them was the curator of the town's historical museum.

Good maps are quite indispensible here. The Forest Service roads are poorly and confusingly marked. The *Leesburg and Blackbird Mountain, Idaho, 15 minute topographic maps* are excellent help; however, the *Salmon National Forest Map* (free) would be an adequate although less detailed navigational aid.

*The main street of the newly ghosted town of Cobalt has a general
store on the right and a recreation hall next door.*

From the Leesburg turnoff,* at the junction of Moccasin
and Napias creeks, a good gravel road continues downstream
about three miles to the point where Panther Creek enters
from the south. The left-hand road reaches up the west
bank of Panther Creek three miles to a narrow flat, totally
occupied by the newly deserted town of Cobalt.

Cobalt, once called Blackbird, is in mint condition. Nothing has been moved and there have been no disastrous fires.
More than one hundred buildings line the streets, standing
white and clean. Except for padlocks and shutters, the town
appears alive and healthy. Cobalt has been deserted since
1959, when the mine closed. Once there were 450 company
employees and a population of more than 2,000. The school
had 120 pupils, 4 teachers and 8 grades. A long three-story
recreation hall stands idly vacant, ready once again to provide entertainment. Next to the hall a long low general

---

*See Leesburg, Idaho.

Each of Cobalt's two bachelors' quarters had twenty-eight rooms and four baths.

store sits empty, its display window boarded over and its round metal IGA sign shot full of holes, none even close to dead center. Most of the buildings are covered with white asbestos shingles and trimmed with green-painted woodwork. The streets are still in fine shape. Occasional manhole covers indicate a drainage system.

How incongruous—a ghost town with manhole covers! No doubt some would argue that a town must be old to be a ghost, but the cold fact is, the town need only be dead. From that moment on, time serves only to age the remains and enhance the memory.

The Blackbird Lode, with its rich deposits of gold, was responsible for the birth and subsequent death of Cobalt. Located two miles up Panther Creek, then another four miles to the right up Blackbird Creek, the buildings at the mine fill the creek's narrow canyon. The town of Blackbird was once located here. Some of the old log cabins still squat beside the stream. One in particular sports a set of over-long

Early-morning mists rise over the Blackbird Mine. Originally a gold mine, it became one of the country's leading producers of cobalt.

ridgepoles, as if a deluxe porch had been planned but never realized.

It was 8:00 A.M. when I drove up the canyon to look over the old site. It was foggy, and I nearly drove through the locked gate blocking the road below the mine. A doorbell-type button offered a chance at access. Shortly, a young mining engineer responded to the signal, and invited me in for a quick tour. He explained that the mine was indeed inactive, but that a crew was drilling test holes, attempting to locate new leads. We talked for a while about the lost veins and new strikes made at the Blackbird.

Gold was found here in 1893. In pursuit of the yellow vein, nickel and copper were found. In 1901 cobalt was found in quantity, but no market existed for the metal. From 1913 to 1921, thirty-five thousand dollars' worth of gold, nickel, and copper was mined. Ore was hauled to Utah for smelting.

The boom arrived in 1939, with a government contract for cobalt. The new town of Cobalt was built, and tons of cobalt ore were yanked out and sold at a guaranteed price of $2.30 per pound. By 1959, fourteen million pounds had been mined. The government contract expired that year, the mine closed, and Cobalt lost its reason for existence. The town was quickly deserted. Later the mine was sold for its junk metal, but the new owner found some copper left and brought it to the surface in '63 and '67. The mine was then resold to the Idaho Copper Mining Company. It is their engineers who are reevaluating the residual deposits.

Metals worth in excess of fifty million dollars have been taken from the tunnels of the Blackbird. For one short moment in its history, it was the world's leader in gold production, and gold was only a sideline to the production of cobalt.

Should investigation reveal new deposits, the mine and town will arise again to full life, probably rechristened for whatever metal is found. "Nickel" has a nice ring to it— but "gold" sounds a shade richer.

Metal parts for the Yellow Jacket Mill were packed in by mule train. Originally a mill with thirty stamps, the number was later increased to sixty.

YELLOW JACKET, IDAHO

It was raining and the light was rapidly fading. The route to Yellow Jacket was long and doubtful. A roadside cafe looked inviting. Perhaps someone there would have information about the roads and the extent of the remains left at Yellow Jacket.

"Yes, there's an old town there—and an old mine. They called it the YJ Mine." The waitress had heard others speak of the place and was happy to pass on the information. "Someone, the other day, said the hotel burned down." This news, the rain, and the prospect of twenty-five miles of soupy roads was reason enough to consider a change in plans.

Had it not been for the chance appearance of a passing fisherman, I would have missed one of the finest and least known ghost towns in Idaho. As the gentleman entered the

Lonely, overwhelmed by forest and sky, the little cabin echoes the
isolation of Yellow Jacket—sixty miles from the nearest city.

A three-foot-diameter Pelton wheel was adequate to power a five-stamp mill. Water under tremendous pressure was directed against the wheel's metal cups.

cafe, the waitress called to him, "Say—didn't that hotel at Yellow Jacket burn down last year?"

"No, that's just rumor—I was down there last week, and it's still there—all five stories."

"Five?" My voice was unnaturally loud.

"Well," he answered, "it's three stories in front and five behind. It's a long son of a gun, but they never quite finished it. Guess it was never used. There's a crew in there now—assessing the old mine."

An hour later I had gathered all the information available from the helpful fisherman, and even received permission from the cafe owner to camp overnight at a nearby deserted trailer park.

By morning the skies cleared. The gravelly soil had absorbed much of the rain, and a brisk wind was quickly evaporating the remainder. The roads were in good shape. Upstream along Panther Creek, seven miles from the cafe at the Blackbird Road Junction, a narrow road branches to the right. Traveling generally west, it climbs along South Fork Creek, switchbacks over the south slope of Quartzite Mountain, repeats its contortions on the down side, joins Shovel Creek and parallels its path downstream. Fifteen miles on this road—about an hour—brings you to the Yellow Jacket Ranger Station. Three miles farther, and over sixty miles from the nearest city, is the old town of Yellow Jacket.

A giant sixty-stamp mill is first in view. Water, conducted downhill through a twenty-four-inch-diameter conduit, with a one-hundred-and-fifty-foot head, provided plenty of power to lift the sixty stamps, each in turn. Inside the mill is a complete smithy.

Nearby are a number of supply sheds, and beyond these are a few old residences, and there—on the grassy knoll— is the hotel! It is indeed three stories high, its upper floor made livable by eighteen dormers. In back—the land slopes down—the imposing wooden structure was just as described, five stories high!

I stopped by an old cabin that seemed lately refurbished to ask permission to snoop about. One of the mining engineers, recently new to the site, volunteered some information.

Placer gold was found in Yellow Jacket Creek by Long Wilson in 1869. Not just fine color, but good-sized nuggets. Many Leesburg miners moved in to stake claims. Later that year, Nathan Smith found the mother lode far up the hill north of camp. It was free gold in quartz, requiring only pulverizing and panning. In 1893, materials for the thirty-stamp mill were packed in by mule train. Later, thirty more stamps were added. The mill is now in disrepair, but structurally sound and capable of reactivation.

During boom years, 1890 to 1900, the population of Yellow Jacket approached two hundred. After 1900, mining dropped off, becoming sporadic in the twenties. In 1932 mining resumed and the prospects looked so good that construction on the hotel was commenced.

Soon prospects faltered as the veins began to pinch out. In desperation, the early tailings were remilled. Mining operations slumped farther in the late thirties, and ceased entirely in 1942. About one million dollars in gold had been

Thirteen rooms in a row, and the miners were a superstitious lot. The hotel was doomed to failure. Not from bad luck, but merely from poor timing. The rich veins and the hotel were finished the same year.

realized from the mine. Now its tunnels and drifts are being core drilled in search of suspected deposits of silver, lead, and copper. Several miners and their families have found temporary quarters in two of the old cabins next to the hotel.

Two of the miners' kids volunteered to conduct a tour of the town. They told me their ages were seven and eleven. That sounded like a good dice score, so I asked if they felt lucky. Their blank stares indicated that I was totally misunderstood. First on the agenda was a visit with the pet rabbits. The older boy explained, "That speckled one is named Mr. Bunny." The younger one added, "And the white one is named Whitey. The third bunny was black, so I speculated aloud that his name was Blacky.

"No," replied the younger one, "we call him Hoppy because of the way he jumps."

The rear of the hotel is five stories high. The white scar along the left side of the windows outlines the location of an "enclosed ladder" fire escape. The young girl standing in the window is the daughter of a miner who is presently doing assessment work at the Yellow Jacket Mine.

I allowed that the names were fitting, and congratulated the two on their originality. Communications firmly established, we proceeded with the tour.

Shortly west of the hotel is a badly dilapidated log and clapboard building. Its function would still be a mystery, except for the metal Pelton wheel mounted on heavy timbers at the downhill end of the structure. Water under great pressure was forced against the metal cups of the Pelton wheel, giving it tremendous rotational speed. The power developed was geared down and fed to a small stamp mill. A five-stamp mill once operated in Yellow Jacket, and this little shack must have housed the works.

Circling back up the hill, the boys pointed out dozens of cabins scattered along the creek and strung out along the road that heads southwest out of town. Many have been used for hunting shacks. Some are too far gone for safe operation. A number of board shacks hidden deep in the shade offered a study in diverse methods of collapse. The boys dubbed them "squashes," "leans," and "bulgers."

Everywhere there were wild snowshoe rabbits. The youngsters pelted away at them with whatever rocks were handy. I mentioned the fact that their pets were close relatives. Their explanation was wholly rational—"We ain't never hit one yet."

The circle completed, we entered the hotel for a detailed inspection The basement, or first floor, was about one-third as long as the hotel, and contained the heating plant, showers, and rudimentary sanitary facilities. The next floor was about two-thirds the length of the hotel and was fitted out as a recreation hall. One old pool table is still there, barren of cloth, its gray slate surface still unbroken. The kitchens are at the back. One huge wood stove has two ovens, two warmers, and room for sixteen pans or twelve big pots. The boys claimed there were seventy-five rooms, with twenty-six more on the top floor that were unfinished. A window count indicated that the estimate was only slightly exaggerated.

At the front of the hotel, a wooden ladder served as fire escape. The rear portion once had a longer ladder with protective hoops. For those lodgers in the center portion, there were knotted ropes tied to bedsteads. In a hurry, you could grab the top knot and leap out the window, then slide down from knot to knot. Care had to be taken not to grab the wrong end of the rope. In such an event, the unfortunate victim would reach the ground and the end of the rope at the same horrible moment.

The builder of the hotel must have had a similar moment of truth when he realized that the mine was petering out just as he was finishing the top floor.

Known to few, and visited by even fewer, the town of Yellow Jacket remains remote and unchanged. Little has been written about the site. Much of its charm is from facts unknown and questions unanswered.

IDAHO AREA 2

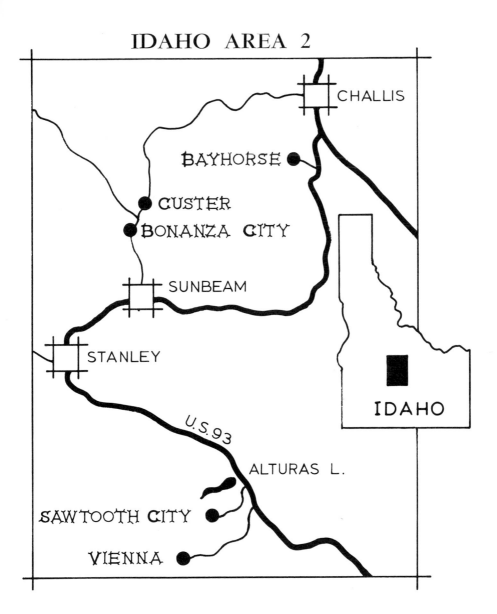

BAYHORSE, IDAHO

NAMED IN 1864 for two bay horses, the proud possessions of an itinerant miner, this tiny gold placer camp was destined to become famous for its hard-rock silver deposits.

The streams in the area may have been named by the same unimaginative folk who christened the camp—Mud Spring,

The Bayhorse Saloon was the most popular spot in town. Fancy rooms above, accessed by private stairway and fronted with a balustraded porch, were easily rented and always occupied.

John Gulch, Birch Creek, Wood Creek, and, of course, Bayhorse Creek. All drain eastward three miles to the Salmon River. Recently the Salmon has been given a second more romantic name. Called the "River of No Return" in song and movie, the new designation was quickly adopted by Idahoans.

Claims were staked on the hillsides above the site of Bayhorse during the early 1870's. Beginning in 1877 tunnels were dug at the Riverview, Bayhorse, Pacific, Ramshorn, Skylark, and Keystone claims. The Ramshorn was the prime producer. Mills and smelters were built, and silver poured forth at a rate of nearly five hundred thousand dollars per year. By 1898 ten million dollars in silver and lead had been mined, milled, and poured into ingots. Another two

Presenting a solid front while sagging at the rear, the green stone company building stands alone, its denuded sign proclaiming abandonment.

and a half million dollars was realized when the mines were reactivated in the 1920's.

Bayhorse is located eleven miles south of Challis on U.S. Highway 93, and three and a half miles west on a good gravel road. The mines are presently inoperative. No current reassessments are being made, but the presence of a caretaker and the heavy metal doors on the company buildings attest to the possibility of future activity. The caretaker lives in what used to be the butcher shop. The next building to the west is the old saloon, with rooms overhead. East of the caretaker's home is the old rock commissary. Originally a company store, this building was put to many uses, serving as post office, newspaper office, and, lastly, a powder house. It was constructed in a craftsmanlike manner of hard green rock. Generally considered rare, the green rock was apparently common in Bayhorse, for most of the company buildings are of like color and construction.

Farther east and across the road is a ramshackle shed totally occupied by a vintage Chevrolet. Although all of its tires are flat, the owner has taken the precaution of preventing theft by wrapping numerous turns of clothesline wire about the car's body, entrapping the hood, doors, and trunk lid.

A large number of slide-rock dugouts are imbedded in the hillside. Some dugouts, built on level land, are head high and well covered with soil. Only the sloping entrances reveal their locations.

The caretaker wasn't too happy to discuss the history of Bayhorse. It was Saturday, and many weekend vacationers were on their way to the Bayhorse Lakes, located five miles west of town. A number of visitors had already interrupted the old-timer's breakfast. He answered my knock, stood guardedly in the doorway, and reluctantly answered my questions. Behind me two station wagons pulled to a dusty halt. Doors flew open and Bayhorse was flooded with dogs, parents, and little people. The caretaker retreated, closing the door firmly behind him. Shortly he reappeared, carrying a box of groceries. He quietly loaded it aboard his pickup and took off. His dog, apparently used to this procedure, met the truck a block away, sized up the vehicle's speed, and made it over the tailgate in one well-timed running leap.

Just above town, past the Bayhorse Mine and mill, and across the creek, are six large charcoal kilns. Wood from miles around was charred in these ovens. Starved of oxygen, the wood became charcoal, which in turn was fired to high temperature in a bellows-fed furnace. The final separation of silver from its concentrate depended upon such intense heat.

Two miles above the kilns, the buildings of the old Ramshorn Mine cling tenaciously to the steep hillside. The Ramshorn had eight tunnels located halfway up the mountain slope. Above the Ramshorn, and two thousand feet above the creek, are the four tunnels of the Skylark Mine. Connecting the two mines, and a loading station at creek level, was a high-capacity tramway. A few cables still cross the sky overhead, and surviving towers can be traced up to skyline. The lower tramway station at creek level was a combination terminal tower, loading bin, and control house.

Charcoal kilns stand intact at the upstream end of town. The large iron pot may have been used to burn lime.

Cast-iron pulley wheels permitted the endless cable to angle downward to the tension-weighted "turn around" wheel. The tramway seems to have been gravity powered. In fact it was perhaps overpowered by gravity at times. Braking the downward movement of the bucket-laden cable was probably the system's primary speed control.

There are three more high-mountain mines near the old town of Bayhorse, all accessible by four wheels or shoe leather. The *Bayhorse, Idaho, 7½ minute* topographic map shows their locations clearly—right down to the individual switchbacks leading to each site.

Two days in Bayhorse were hardly long enough to soak up the scenery. Another three to explore, two more, perhaps, to test the trout, and I would have been almost willing to face civilization.

The lower tramway station at the Bayhorse Mine stands fractured
and fallen. The turn-around wheel was mounted on a weighted
lever that provided the cables with the proper tension.

The Yankee Fork dredge, still intact and floating, is one of the last remnants of the placering effort at Bonanza.

BONANZA CITY, IDAHO

The salmon were starting their run, and the "River of No Return" was lined with fishermen. Every campground was full, from Challis to Clayton to Sunbeam. The campgrounds located along the three-mile stretch of river below Sunbeam were particularly crowded.

I stopped at a favored fishing hole, densely populated with anglers, to observe the methods used and perhaps share in the excitement that comes with the hooking of a big fish. Just below the fishermen, the river was comparatively shallow. Called "Indian Riffles," it was a good place to watch for moving salmon. Occasionally an observer would shout and point to a big one rolling in the white water, and the expectations of the fishermen above would temporarily rise.

Metal roofing blown askew, stovepipe disjointed, ravaged by the elements—but still standing. An old cabin at the south edge of Bonanza.

"Fish on," the man hollered, and everyone pulled in his line to give the hooked fish room to run. Advice was plentiful. The fishermen already constituted a crowd. Now more moved in to watch the action. Seldom hooked deeply, most salmon manage to throw the hook on their thrashing airborne excursions. But this angler was talented. He "bent" the fish over at its every attempt to break the surface. Soon two men moved in with large landing nets. The fisherman led the tired salmon, flat side up, into the closest net, and the fifteen-pound beauty was lifted safely to dry land. A cheer went up, and a dozen anxious fishermen, their hopes again raised, recast their lures into the water.

I resumed my trek up the river, paralleling the course of the migrating salmon. There was more excitement in the campgrounds now. A salmon had been caught, the run was on—the word was spreading!

A few minutes later I stopped at the cafe in Sunbeam for a cup of coffee. As I entered, a dozen men hurriedly paid

Tin can chinking decorates the front of this residence. Once a store on the main street, it was fronted with a stout boardwalk and hitching rail.

their bills and left. One of the few remaining customers turned to me and volunteered, "Did you hear about the twenty-five pounder they caught down at Indian Riffles?"

Perhaps word of the gold strikes of a century ago had

spread in the same way. Seemingly, word covered ground
faster than a man could travel. Gold was, in fact, discovered
at this spot where the Yankee Fork joins the Salmon; however, the richest deposits were found a few miles upstream
on Yankee Fork.

Heaved to the surface long ago by some gigantic igneous
belch, veins of gold-bearing ore, exposed to the air, slowly
softened and eroded. Finely divided particles of the rich
yellow metal traveled for miles down the turbulent waters
of the Yankee Fork. Excited miners found the color and
followed the trail back upstream, noting carefully the
amount of gold found in each pan. If suddenly the colors
(specks of gold) were lessened, it meant only that exposed
veins were nearby. Somewhere above, on the right or left
bank, could be found the mother lode that had spawned
the yellow trace.

W. A. Norton found the first rich outcropping in 1875.
Named the "Charles Dickens," the lode gave up $11,500 in
gold during the first month. The richness of the mine and
the promise of more deposits in the area were reason enough
to build a town. A gently sloping spot on the west bank of
Yankee Fork was selected. Just eight miles north of the
present site of Sunbeam, the new town was centrally located
among the more promising claims. First there were just a
store and saloon, then in 1879 a newspaper, and by 1880 a
population of fifteen hundred.

Bonanza City* it was called. Soon a two-story hotel and
a dance hall were constructed. Bonanza's three main
streets were quickly filled with buildings. In five years the
peak was reached—and the death knell sounded when a
stamp mill was built at the General Custer Mine, two miles
north. A new town sprang up at its side, and Bonanza
shrank as the town of Custer swelled.

It has been quiet in Bonanza for the past sixty years, except for the dredging operation of the forties and early
fifties. Wandering up the stream, the mammoth machine
scratched out nearly two million in gold from seven miles
of the Yankee Fork's bed. The dredge is still there, and now
both it and the town are quiet.

A dozen buildings stand vacant, some quite sound and recently in repair. One old shack at the south end of town is
covered with "roll" roofing. Long thin sheets of galvanized

---

*See Custer for map information.

Enlarged at random, a small log cabin has become one of the larger homes in Bonanza.

iron are haphazardly attached to the double log roof. Winds have picked up the loose ends of some of the metal strips and rolled them up in awkward curves. Bedsprings lean against an outside wall, while inside, a low, wooden, boxed-in area is filled with straw. The walls are papered with old "photogravures," some dated 1922.

In the center of town a number of buildings, stand in a neat row, connected at their fronts by a rotting wooden boardwalk. One of these structures displays evidence of laborious repair, designed to prevent the unwanted ingress of winter's icy blast. Where the plaster chinking was cracked and loose, flattened tin cans were tacked on in windproof overlapping rows. Across the street a stout but windowless home displays a copper-sheeted roof. Originally a simple log structure, it has been enlarged with clapboard additions. Slanted shed roofs extend in three directions, giving the old house a dignified appearance, however accidental.

To the north, an imposing peak dominates the skyline. Named "Bald Mountain," its barren, rounded top gives it the appearance of age. It seems to look down, with a compassion born of like circumstance, upon the elderly homes and deserted streets of Bonanza City.

The protection of a copper-clad roof has enabled the Custer school to survive years of abandonment. Filled with artifacts of the mining era, it is now one of the finest mining-camp museums of its kind in the country.

CUSTER, IDAHO

In 1876, just one year after the discovery of the Charles Dickens Lode near the site of Bonanza, three prospectors, Baxter, Dodge, and McKein, located a vein of greater promise. Named the "General Custer," it lasted about as long, and expired with the same glory as its colorful namesake.

No exploratory work was needed since the vein was long, thick, and exposed. Enough ore was in sight to warrant construction of a mill. Four years of contested claims and litigation ensued. In 1879, a California combine bought up the primary claims, including the "General Custer" and the nearby "Unknown" and started construction of a mill. The metal wheels, shafts, and stamps were hauled in by pack-train. The thirty-stamp mill completed, processing of ore commenced in 1880. Mill workers and miners moved in from Bonanza. Some even moved entire homes up the two-mile stretch of nearly level road.

The first year, more than one million dollars was realized from the General Custer Mine. By 1886, Custer had grown to nearly thirty-five hundred, but the inevitable bad news was quietly spreading. The ore was reducing in grade, containing less gold per ton. The owners (or creditors) of the General Custer and the Charles Dickens unloaded their properties on some willing British buyers, who in turn capitalized the operation with a stock issue. The new company lasted until 1892, its collapse spelling the end of the first lode-mining boom. Of the thirteen million dollars in gold and silver taken from the Yankee Fork mines, the General Custer had been responsible for seven million dollars.

Three years later, a new vein was found near the old Custer tunnels. Dubbed the "Lucky Boy," it released another million dollars' worth of gold in nine years. As the mine deepened, the cost of hoisting out the ore rose, and in 1904 the Lucky Boy was forced to close down. The same year a new find on Jordan Creek resulted in formation of the Sunbeam Company, and subsequent construction of a new mill. Its rich ores petered out during enlargement of facilities, and in 1911 the Sunbeam Company also failed. The town of Custer, already largely depopulated, quickly became a ghost.

The old schoolhouse stands lonely in a small clearing at the north edge of town, its metal-coated hip roof offering stubborn protection. The bell and cupola are gone. Scars above the door show their earlier presence. The slate boards and school seats have been removed. In their places are the tools and treasures that marked the greatness of Custer's yesterday. The old schoolhouse is now one of the finest mining-camp museums in the country. There is an abundance of old gold rockers, wheelbarrows, hand tools, skips (ore hoist buckets), along with a variety of early household appliances.

The doctor's house and the old McKensie residence stand together, the lone remnants of a row of buildings that once crowded the main street of Custer. Its porch sagging and held static by temporary supports, the old doc's house shows signs of being used later as a community store. Lettering over the porch roof is visible, but not readable. Apparently as an afterthought, a heater and stovepipe were added, the

The "old doc's" house, with the McKensie residence beyond. The pot on top of the stovepipe prevents an invasion by squirrels and chipmunks.

stovepipe extending through the transom above the old double doors. The stovepipe rises high above the ridge of the
roof, and is thoughtfully capped with an old pot, effectively
shutting off one means of access favored by enterprising
rodents.

Nothing but an ore bin is left at the site of the General
Custer Mill, but nearby, an old deserted home shows a hint
of finery. Fancied up with embossed galvanized sheets, and
papered with intricately patterned oilcloth, it probably was
once the home of a top company official.

I would have liked to explore the hillsides near Custer
and Bonanza, but the maps detailing the area had disappeared. It had been windy, and I had left the truck windows open. Assuredly, the maps had blown away. Three
weeks later, and some six hundred miles removed from the
site, I found them crumpled and creased, cowering in the
crevasse of the front seat. Belated inspection showed a
number of locations I should have visited, such as The Lucky
Boy Camp, about three air miles east of Bonanza. The camp
has eleven tunnels, thirteen shafts, and sixteen buildings
indicated on the map. A half mile up Jordan Creek are the
tunnels of the Charles Dickens, and four miles farther, the
buildings of the Sunbeam and Montana mines. All are
clearly shown on the *7½ minute Sunbeam and Custer, Idaho,*
topographic maps, along with numerous prospect sites and
unidentified deserted buildings. The road past the Sunbeam
Mine follows Jordan Creek, switchbacks over Loon Creek
Summit, then runs down the west fork of Mayfield Creek to
the old placer camps on Loon Creek. It was over this pass
known for its deep and treacherous snows, that many prospectors traveled on their quest for gold on the Yankee Fork.
Some day I will travel that path, with maps firmly in hand.

The wagon-sized door of the old blacksmith shop was narrowed to man-size when the building was converted to living quarters. Braced from falling, the structure slowly decays downward.

SAWTOOTH CITY, IDAHO

The old log buildiing leans heavily to the side, relying gratefully upon the strength of a sturdy pine that has grown closely by its flank. A pole is wedged against the front of the aged structure. Downward is the only direction left to this final surviving remnant of Sawtooth City. The cabin was built about 1880, when the tree alongside was yet to be seeded. Once a busy blacksmith's shop at the east end of the main street, its double doors were originally wide enough to admit team and wagon. The door was narrowed to normal width at the convenience of some later resident. A few more cheerless ruins are sprinkled along the main thoroughfare, their logs slanting to a peak at resistant corners. The logs are bleached and cracked. Soft to the finger, they cannot last for long.

*A few interlocking corners still mark the sites of the once sturdy log
homes scattered along the main cross street of Sawtooth City.*

Sawtooth City* is just a few miles west of U.S. Highway
93. A well-signed road exits to the west about one mile south
of the Alturas Lake Road. Heading up Beaver Creek, it is
joined in two miles by a road coming in from the left. Sawtooth City's cemetery is high on a barren hill north of the
junction. The townsite is a mile or so farther up Beaver
Creek.

Sawtooth was once a lively town, with a population approaching one thousand. In 1882 its two intersecting streets
held twenty-five homes, three saloons, two eating houses,
three stores, a livery, an assay office, a meat market, and of
course the sturdy log smithy.

*See Vienna for map information.

New rope on old crosses shows that someone cares.
Nature quickly reclaims what man forgets.

In 1879, the ruby silver had been spotted in quartz out-crops by Levi Smiley. Within two years nine rich veins of the same antimonial silver had been found and claimed. One of the more active mines was the Pilgrim, with its 1,200-foot tunnel and ores running as rich as 5,000 ounces of silver per ton. The Silver King, two miles up Beaver Creek, was the most productive, and the most persistently active. It was a small town by itself, complete with bunkhouse and mill.

Still sporadically active, the Silver King has suffered through a number of ownerships, setbacks, and disasters. A fire in 1891 destroyed its shaft work, hoist house, and air and water pumps. Although the Silver King endured, its limited production was not enough to keep Sawtooth City alive. Less than ten years after it was founded, the town was deserted, and the towering peaks of the Sawtooth Range assumed silent guardianship.

Dead, barkless branches arch over sagging cabin walls. This is one of many time-worn relics at Vienna City.

VIENNA, IDAHO

Just over the hill and up Smiley Canyon, the sprawling camp called "Vienna" was a short eight miles by stage from its sister community of Sawtooth City. Relations between the two towns were strained, and at times were near the feuding point. Each had its own stage line making daily runs between the two towns. Passengers sat lightly in their seats whenever rival coaches met. The encounters were mostly verbal, punctuated with an occasional whiplash aimed at the opposition's horses.

The towns were remarkably similar. Each had its own mill, and a nearly equal number of mines. Sawtooth City had its Silver King Mine, and Vienna had its Vienna Mine. Both were discovered by the Smiley group that explored the area in 1879. Vienna developed a year or two behind Sawtooth, but grew to several times its size. In 1882 Vienna had three stores, fourteen saloons, six eateries, a small one-man furniture factory, and a newspaper with two hundred supporters. Flagged the *Vienna Reporter*, it sold two hundred subscriptions for $1.50 each. Within five months the editor sold out to the *Ketchum Keystone*, its prime rival. Like Sawtooth, Vienna's life was short, and by 1914 nearly all of its two hundred buildings had been moved or torn down. Only a few log structures were left undisturbed.

The gravel road to Vienna is well surfaced, but difficult to locate. Driving south on Highway 93, the first road to the right, short of Smiley Creek, leads crookedly to the Vienna Road. The turnoff is about four miles south of the Alturas Lake Road. The *Alturas Lake, Marshal Peak* and *Frenchman Creek, Idaho, 7½ minute* topographic maps show the routes in to Sawtooth City and Vienna, and also indicate the locations of the many mines in the area.

The eight-mile drive to the site of Vienna is of singular beauty. Lined with lodgepole pines for much of the way, the road frequently breaks out into small parklike openings, often occupied by mule deer. Jagged tops of the Sawtooth Range break the horizon, closing in as the valley narrows. Vienna occupies the last wide spot, just beyond the second crossing of Smiley Creek.

The surviving traces of Vienna are sprinkled downstream along the north bank. Hidden among the trees are numerous old remnants of civilization, much like those of Sawtooth City. Long dead, the two cities still retain their twinship.

Some cabins are built of logs hewn on all four sides. Such fancy construction is seldom found in old mining camps. One log structure has been reduced to a rectangular outline, low on the ground, with a doorframe projecting nearly vertical. A dead tree stands nearby, its whitened limbs gnarled and randomly twisted.

Shortly upstream and adjacent to the road are the foundations of an old mill. One-half mile farther, the road branches. The left branch leads to the old Vienna Mine. The right fork goes a short distance and dead ends at a ford that has been inundated by a mud flow. The area above is soupy from spring water, and has caused fine sucking mud and gravel to roll slowly downhill. In this area, even

A two-story log structure of undetermined use, located at the old
Webfoot Mine above Vienna City. A built-in outhouse
with vapor vent nestles in the near corner.

walking is hazardous. A few hundred yards above the flow
are the remains of the Webfoot Mine. Appropriately named,
the most reliable footing was underground. The mine has
a number of structures. A few are intact—an old smithy,
and a large structure of uncertain use. The large building
was once two stories high, with a full basement underneath.
Too collapsed to permit full exploration, it seemed from
the outside to have been a dormitory. I could find no shafts
or tunnels, although the building's wreckage could easily
have hidden them. At the uphill end was a lean-to, and next
to it a small built-in outhouse with chimney-style vapor
vent.

Approximately one-half mile uphill from the Webfoot is
the old Vienna shaft. Presently it is being reworked by

Rudely askew, sections of old buildings at the Webfoot Mine create a disorientation countered only by the reliably vertical trees in the background.

the Heinecke Company. They are under contract to cut a thirteen-hundred-foot tunnel and run twenty-five hundred feet of side drifts. Should these workings uncover the expected veins, a new mill will be built and the ore reduced to concentrate, which will be sent out to be smeltered. Tests have shown silver, lead, zinc, and gold to be present. Past activities of the Vienna have produced over one million dollars in silver and gold.

With a little luck, the Vienna may exceed the Silver King of rival Sawtooth City. The towns no longer vie for leadership, but their two leading mines carry out the feud like a pair of boxers, dead on their feet but still swinging.

IDAHO AREA 3

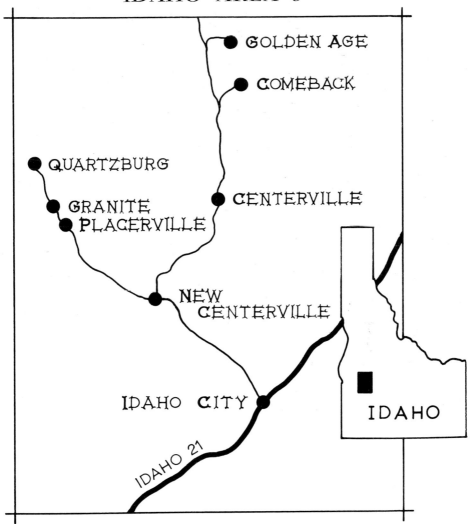

GOLDEN AGE

COMEBACK

QUARTZBURG

GRANITE
PLACERVILLE

CENTERVILLE

NEW
CENTERVILLE

IDAHO CITY

IDAHO 21

IDAHO

IDAHO CITY, IDAHO

GREATER THAN the Alaska Klondike! Richer than the California Rush of '49! The eighteen-square-mile area called Boise Basin, surrounding the town of Idaho City, is said to have delivered two hundred and fifty million dollars in gold. So state the members of the Idaho City Historical Foundation. Other historians have estimated a lesser amount, but

A small portion of Idaho City, as seen looking to the northwest. The white building in the center is the old courthouse.

all agree that square mile for square mile, the placers of the basin were the richest found in North America.

Located at the junction of Mores Creek and Elk Creek, and bounded on three sides by the gulches named Slaughterhouse, Walla Walla, and Warm Springs, the boom town of Idaho City stretched for nearly four miles along the gold-rich streams.

Established in 1862 and named Bannock, it grew to six thousand souls the first year. In 1864 the territorial legislature incorporated the settlement as Idaho City. For twenty years it was the largest town in the territory. Once there were over ten thousand residents (some estimates run as high as thirty thousand) in the city, half of them Oriental. The lure of new-found gold on Loon Creek caused the town to shrink a bit in the 1870's, but hard-rock mining and dredging sustained Idaho City until 1942, when gold production was curtailed by the government.

In 1968, the sign at the edge of town read "pop 188." Residents claim only one hundred and twenty-two live year round in Idaho City—and most of those are forest rangers or loggers.

A few old-timers, still actively mining, add to the town's

Portable three-stamp mill on display at the open-air museum. Ore was placed in the hopper at the rear, which fed it into the stamps. Any ore not crushed fine was sent through a second time.

atmosphere. Hollow footsteps resound as bearded "hard rockers" saunter down the wooden boardwalks of Main Street. The walks are so thoroughly used, especially around the old courthouse, that the thick planks have been worn thin. High spots caused by the resistance of nails and knots

Home of Idaho Territory's largest newspaper of the 1880's. The storefront, typical of most in Idaho City, is complete with covered boardwalk and "sittin' bench."

have left the walk bumpy to the point that strangers find it awkward to maintain a steady course.

Forty-six saloons once sold the products of Idaho City's four breweries. Five of the saloons had fancy billiard rooms. Only one of the hard liquor dispensaries has survived. Originally called the "Miners' Exchange Saloon," it has been renamed, but continues to peddle the same reliable merchandise. Saloons are generally fruitful places to gather information. Close-lipped old-timers are often more talka-

Handwrought hinges and homemade square nails made escape from this territorial prison difficult. The jail, dismantled and moved from its original location, was reassembled and the doors merely tacked in place. One of the doors was placed "wrong side to."

tive under the influence of minor amounts of "Tongue oil."

I entered the old saloon intending to quaff a short salute to the rich history of Idaho City, but the maps that I had brought in with me caused a delay in plans. Before I realized it, the maps were pulled from my grasp and spread all over the bar. Miners and loggers alike were pointing out places of interest. The detail present in the 7½ minute maps permits even the most remote shack or tunnel to be located. The

Idaho City, Idaho, 7½ minute topographic map covers the area surrounding the town. I mentioned I was looking for ghost towns—especially the little-known sites.

"There, that's Comeback Mine. You ought to go there. They got a bunkhouse—big two-story thing. Used to be a bunch of people living there."

Another miner chimed in. "Yeah, we're workin' one of the tunnels up there. Come on up anytime. If we're not around, just flip the switch at the tunnel and we'll see the lights flicker. Be glad to show you the place."

The dozen helpful map enthusiasts concluded that I should visit the Bellshazzar, the Comeback, and the Golden Age camps. Of course, I was reminded, Idaho City and Placerville were too big and too interesting to be ignored. Finally, after nearly an hour, the maps were folded, and the glorious past of Idaho City was dutifully honored.

The morning's early light shone brightly on the old Idaho World Building, where the territory's leading paper was published. A big black Labrador retriever insisted on being in every picture I took. It was a quiet and peaceful scene. It wasn't always so. In 1863 the paper reported:

> Several parties were found in the streets Tuesday morning. Some with fractured skulls; some with bunged eyes and swollen faces, indicating very clearly that there had been a muss somewhere during the night. Blood was freely sprinkled about the town on woodpiles and sidewalks. As the puddles of blood were distributed over a large district, it was impossible to locate the fight.

Idaho City had problems concerning adequate law enforcement. The vigilante movement which spread throughout the West is said to have originated here. Seldom did vigilantes apprehend a culprit without rapidly deciding his guilt and applying the quick justice of the rope. For those whose guilt was less than strongly suspect, there was a sturdy jail for temporary durance. Acclaimed the first territorial penitentiary, the convincingly stout building has easily survived to the present. Although moved from its initial site, it is otherwise little changed. The walls of the twenty-by-twenty-four stronghold are constructed of squared logs, twelve inches on a side, and lined with one-inch boards nailed every three inches in all directions, with old-fashioned square nails. Inside partitions, nearly as rugged, are built of four-inch timbers sandwiched between one-inch boards. Deeply carved over one of the cell doors are the words "PRIVET ROOM." Below this sign, state-

The white front of the Masonic Hall—the oldest west of the Mississippi
—contrasts greatly with the unpainted board-and-batten sides. The
stairway was built externally to insure safe exit in case of fire.

ments of a more ribald nature stand for all to read. One
dirty ditty leaves little doubt concerning one prisoner's
opinion of Judge Bear's moral character.

In spite of the two disastrous fires that destroyed much
of the original Idaho City, there are still dozens of old buildings that are worthy of inspection. The Masonic Hall with
its white front and covered stairway is one of the finest.
Propped on both sides and through-bolted with twenty-four-
foot rods, it appears crippled, but well braced. Built in
1865, it looks able to function for another century.

Just west of the center of town, and up the hill to the
north, Boot Hill Cemetery overlooks the modern airstrip
used by local smoke jumpers. Far more bodies rest atop this
hill than are ever found moving along the streets below.
Many of the graves are enclosed with wooden fences, elab-
orately constructed. They now show the sad neglect of time

*Many of the graves on Boot Hill are occupied by large conifers.
Headboards and fences are ruthlessly crowded
aside by the nearly century-old trees.*

and the unemotional encroachment of nature. Massive
trees grow from forgotten graves, crowding headboards
aside, yet—in return—creating beauty from the bitter soil
of death.

Life races on, and the log-truck drivers still wheel their
rigs downhill as if the Reaper were close behind and gaining.

One driver in Idaho City took offense at my suggestion
that loggers by nature were insane and bent on self-destruc-
tion. With jaw muscles tight, he explained that it took three
loads a day to make a living, and that too much slowing
down wore the brake shoes out. "Besides that," he stated,
"I enjoy canning that old semi down the road." Then, eye-
brows lowered, he turned and glared at me with his good
eye, while his off eye burned a hole in the ceiling.

The Magnolia Saloon, fanciest drinking parlor in Placerville, offered
the convenience of a well built into the corner of the porch. The
town ruffian is said to have baited a prospector into going
for his gun by throwing water in his face, then
claiming (successfully) that he killed
the man in self-defense.

PLACERVILLE, IDAHO

Grassy rolling hills, bounded by heavy stands of pine,
form an idyllic setting for the quiet town of Placerville. On
the west bank of a stream carrying the unlikely name of
"Woof Creek," the site overlooks the rich placer beds of
Ophir Creek and Mud Flat.

The *Placerville, Idaho, 7½ minute map* indicates that the
town was incorporated as a square, one full mile on a side.
At its largest, with a population of five thousand, the town
occupied only a fraction of its assigned area, but its boun-
daries included several placer mines which may have alle-
viated the tax burden.

Like a small Midwestern town, Placerville was planned
around a city park, or plaza. The park was surrounded by
business places, with residences forming the perimeter.

A shy old gentleman living just off the plaza was tickled
to have someone to visit with. "It's pretty lonely here," he
told me, "but that's the way I like it."

The front door, one window, and a planter—freshly painted—
demonstrate the meager extent of repair given
this venerable relic of Placerville.

We looked over the surviving business places, especially the old Magnolia Saloon, once the proudest of the town's three drinking parlors. Built in 1900, the Magnolia had a full-width front porch with a built-in well. Like a drinking fountain might function today, the well was a popular gathering spot on hot summer days. The second floor of the saloon was finished, but never used.

The old-timer watched me write down notes as he talked. He asked me not to use his name, and declined to have his picture taken. Perhaps he had a past that was better forgotten.

Across the street, the Boise Basin Mercantile stood empty and tightly shuttered.

"See those metal doors and them shutters? That's all that saved the old store. Had a fire here in—must have been thirty-one, burned a lot of the town. Big forest fire. Burned up the whole town of Quartzburg over west a mile."

The store had a metal roof and plastered walls. I speculated that everyone fled town during the fire.

"No. In fact some men stayed in the old store. Got kinda tense when the ca'tridges next to the wall started goin' off."

The brick butcher shop next to the mercantile survived rather accidentally. The roof burned, but the building proper was saved due to the twelve-inch layer of dirt that had been placed in the ceiling as insulation.

The Emmanuel Episcopal Church stands proud but little used.
Note the painfully decorative shingles.

One store is still in operation, and has been since 1874, twelve years after the town was founded. One can find a little bit of most anything within its dim interior.

A number of fine old homes are scattered about town, some with gingerbread eaves, others with rock wall terraces, showing past pride and recent neglect. The Emmanuel Episcopal Church displays some of the early glory with its arched shingle-covered eaves. Close inspection shows that the shingles were patterned in four subtle ways and tacked in rows to form a design balanced equally on the right and left.

A few new vacation homes are springing up. Impertinent A-frames in shiny colors insult the quiet dignity of the unpainted derelicts that stand magnificent in the town of Placerville.

Adit house and covered trackway of the first tunnel overlooking the Comeback Mining Camp. The tunnel was known for pockets or kidneys of high-grade ore, thickly shot with gold.

COMEBACK MINING CAMP, IDAHO

Tracking down old mining camps can be exciting, rewarding and disgusting. The road leading to the Belshazzar was gated and locked. Bold signs proclaimed the dangers of trespass. The Mayflower Mine had been bought up and converted to vacation homes. The Richland never was much, and now was even less.

The Comeback Camp was as different as it was hard to reach. Between Idaho City and Placerville, at a junction called New Centerville, a gravel road extends northward along Grimes Creek. Three miles from the junction is the town of Centerville, and five miles farther, are the few remaining buildings of Pioneerville, the first town to spring up in Boise Basin. It was known for a time as "Fort

*The two-story bunkhouse with built-in cookshack was littered with old
magazines and mining periodicals. Nearby are an old bachelor's
cabin and a second-level tunnel entrance.*

Hog'em," after the early settlers that hogged the best claims.
Two miles farther north at the second gulch, a "road"
branches to the right. Narrow, washed out, and overhung
with brush, the mile-long trail to Comeback is best suited
to Jeeps and horses.

*Eight-sided water tower just below the Comeback Mine is constructed
of two-by-six lumber laid up flat. Presently it serves
as an ultra-stout power-line pole.*

At the first switchback, a small flat area is occupied by a bachelor's shack, a family residence, machine shop, chicken house, and an old shed with an excavated grease pit. At the uphill side, mine dumps encroach upon the already crowded flat. Above, at the second switchback, a tunnel entrance is capped with a combination machine and tool shed. A long covered trackway braced with logs extends several hundred feet to the end of the mine dump. Recalling the invitation offered by the miners back in Idaho City, I began a search for the light switch I was to flick as a signal of my arrival. No switch was evident, and the tunnel didn't look recently used.

High above was another dump. Perhaps the currently used tunnel was there. I walked up to the "third level" and found another tunnel which also appeared inactive. Next to it, however, was a dilapidated two-story bunkhouse with built-in cookshack. Alongside was an old miner's shack, with barking dog. Above were more tunnels, but no switches, and no sign of life.

Louis Truger, now living in Centerville, was a part owner of the Comeback from 1931 until recently. He stated that over $670,000 in gold had been taken from the tunnels. During 1940 and 1941, an especially rich kidney, or pocket, was uncovered. It yielded nearly $200,000 in gold. During the heyday at the Comeback, twenty-five people stayed on the site, leaving only on weekends to "raise a little hell" in Idaho City.

The mine was found in 1924 by a logger named Louis Painich, who spotted rich mineralization in the soil exposed by an uprooted tree. He took a sample and planned—if it assayed rich—to come back. It was, and he did. He also named the mine.

On my way down the hill I noticed the tire tracks I had made coming up. In places, they were within inches of the steep drop-off. Playing it safe, I crowded the brush-covered "up" side, and promptly collapsed the right mirror and sheared off the radio antenna.

I don't plan to "Comeback."

If you plan to visit the site, drive a narrow vehicle and take along the *Pioneerville, 7½ minute* and *Garden Valley, Idaho, 15 minute* topographic maps.

*The kids walked a mile a day going to and from the Diana School.
School lasted after the mine closed, the teacher having
the pick of the deserted homes.*

GOLDEN AGE CAMP, IDAHO

Placer gold was found along Grimes Creek in 1862. Most of the early miners chose to separate the fine gold laboriously from its attendant sand and gravel. Others, spurning the assurance of a small poke, gambled for higher stakes. Somewhere upstream would be the mother lode.

In classic style, the placers played out as the hard-rock mines were discovered and developed. The Comeback, Missouri, Oro, and the Golden Age mines all tapped residual lodes that had enriched Grimes Creek.

A man named Wells found the richest ore, just four miles north of Pioneerville. Named the Golden Age, the claim eventually became the property of a large Spokane outfit. The ore seemed to get richer with depth, and soon two mills, a dozen homes, two bunkhouses, a recreation hall, and a two-story hotel were built. Seventy-five men worked here during the boom years of the early 1900's. A schoolhouse was

Main Street at the Golden Age Camp is fronted on the right by Grimes Creek, and on the left by two barracks and a hotel. Heavy tar paper was used in lieu of paint and calk.

constructed nearby. Named the "Diana School," it served all the kids of the mining camp. A small outhouse stands behind, and above its narrow door, an overlarge sign states: "MAIN ENTRANCE."

The *Garden Valley, Idaho, 15 minute* map shows the locations of both the school and mining camp.

An eighty-one-year-old former miner named Hawkins is now the caretaker. He and his wife live in one of the residences at the camp. We toured the empty camp, carefully inspecting the larger buildings. The second story of the hotel contained the main company offices, and a large dance hall. The men were paid three dollars a day, with one dollar per day deducted for room and board. Saturday was payday, and Saturday night was for dancing. The big bosses could sit in their offices and watch benevolently over their cavorting employees. The downstairs portion of the hotel contained a dining hall, a small company store, a few rooms and a large kitchen with built-in woodshed. A huge Arcadian range filled one end of the kitchen. A fifty-gallon drum was adapted as a side-arm heater, with coils extending into and around the old stove.

For a while the mills turned out thirty-five hundred dollars in gold per day. The deep vein made removal of ore difficult, and when the shaft went below creek level, the water flooded in. The cost of lifting and processing the ore,

Not so private privy is located behind the Diana School

combined with the added expense of pumping the water, more than equaled the value of the gold. The mine shut down. Before long, both mills and some of the camp structures burned to the ground.

No one knows how much gold is left in the hill. It is under water. But, as Hawkins stated, "Gold doesn't dissolve, you know."

PART IV
WYOMING

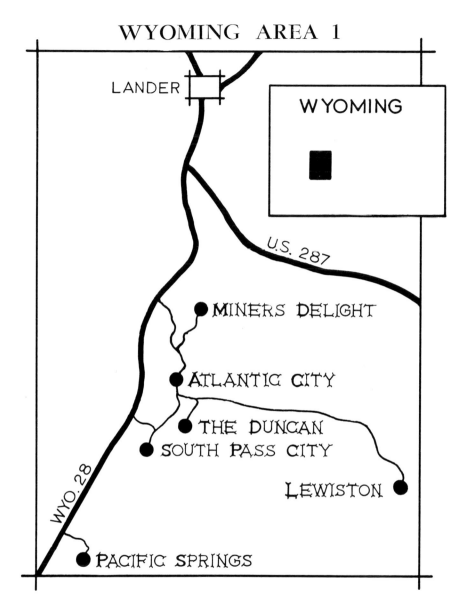

ATLANTIC CITY, WYOMING

PERCHED ATOP the high flats of the South Pass, on the easiest route across the Rockies, are the ghostly remains of a half dozen century-old towns. Towns that grew to a total population of more than five thousand in two short years, to die slowly from the disappointment of pinched-out veins, and

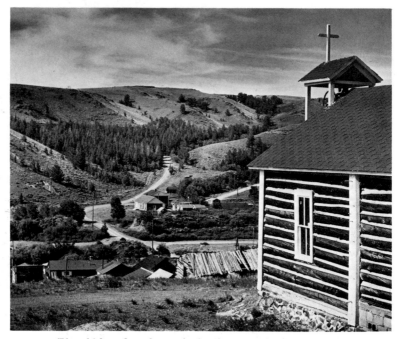

*The old log church overlooks the sprawling remains of the once
booming town of Atlantic City. The Carpenter
Hotel stands in the background.*

sands "too poor to pan." Atlantic City and South Pass City
were like fraternal twins. The same age, the same size, but
Atlantic was wild and South Pass was tame. A third town,
Miners Delight, threatened to overshadow all others with
the richest mine in the whole Sweetwater area. Pacific
Springs and Lewiston both blossomed from small way stations on the combined Emigrant and Oregon Trails. On a
nearby hill was a community built around a mine. It was
seldom given the status of a town, but the dignity of its
name, The Duncan, implied much more than just a mine.
With its own dormitory, mill, and smelter, it had everything
but women, and later that shortage was remedied.

Atlantic City and South Pass were both founded about the
same time, and old-timers still argue as to which town came
into prominence first. All agree that South Pass City was
the historical seat of the state of Wyoming.

"After all, they had the first woman Justice of the Peace
in the whole United States."

*These ten stamps were once kept busy crushing gold-bearing ore.
Powered by a steam engine, each stamp was lifted
by the camshaft and dropped in turn.*

Courtesy Jerrie Moerer Collection, Atlantic City, Wyo.
The old rock building, as it was in 1893. The second-floor dancing parlor was reportedly operated by Calamity Jane. A minor earthquake some years ago reduced the building to one story.

"But Atlantic City had the first brewery, the first beer garden, the largest dance hall, and the finest opera house in the area—and them's in order of importance, too, son."

During the year of 1867, the population of Atlantic City reached nearly three hundred. That was the year of the big discovery. The "Atlantic Ledge," it was called. Several feet thick and thousands of feet long, it slanted sharply into the ground, but was tracked down by a hundred shafts, and its gold-bearing quartz brought to the revealing light of the sun. Free-milling gold it was, needing only crushing and mechanical separation. The boom was on! By 1869, the population of Atlantic City was nearly two thousand. Dozens of stamp mills were laboriously hauled the long route from the Union Pacific line nearly one hundred miles to the

Courtesy Jerrie Moerer Collection, Atlantic City, Wyo.
Emil Granier and his chief engineer, W. G. Peters, scan the hillside,
planning the route of the famous twenty-mile Christina Ditch.
The project was a monumental failure. The photo-
graph was taken in the early 1880's.

south. In three year's time, the town had grown to respectability. A log school was built. A large stone building was constructed by J. W. Anthony and operated as a store by Robert McAuley. It was a two-story achievement, the upper story extending back into the hillside to form more than ninety feet of dance hall. It was here that Calamity

Carefully braced and lovingly restored, the old log church at Atlantic City is still used during the summer months. It is considered a classic of early-1900 architecture.

The old livery clings to the slope, sagging and leaning. It is collapsing from the inside, and the building is unsafe to enter. An old residence is in the background.

Jane carried out (or arranged for) some of her numerous enterprises.

In 1862, Emil Granier, a French engineer with foreign capital, proposed a twenty-mile sluiceway to bring water in from the northern watershed. The ditch was built with one thousand dollars and "six tons of sweat from three hundred Swedes." The ditch passed through many miles of hard rock, wound its way to a point above town, circled around it on the contour, and angled south. A number of wooden sluices bridged the gullies and canyons. Christina Lake, at the head of the ditch, was dammed to create a vast water supply. The gates were opened and the waters rushed forth —a bit too fast—for the grade had been laid out with too much slope. Sluices were wiped out and the waters spilled over. Every miner in the area rushed in to use the unexpected supply of "liquid gold." In every gully and wash, minor bonanzas were uncovered. The consumption of whiskey hit a new high, and saloons were filled with miners

The one-hundred-year-old Rose Mine, located two miles north of
Atlantic City, overlooks the modern iron extraction facilities
of the United States Steel Corporation.

celebrating their new-found wealth. The defeated Emil
Granier returned to France to explain, and, hopefully, to
refinance the operation. He was promptly jailed, tried, and
sentenced to life imprisonment!

In spite of the Granier ditch failure, Atlantic City was
far from dead. Mr. Giessler built a new store in 1898. The
Carpenter family constructed a large two-story log hotel
in 1900. A rodeo was held on Main Street that year to cele-
brate the Fourth of July. In 1912 the log church was built,
later to be dignified with the label of "National Shrine."

Most of the gold had been taken by 1875, and by 1920
nearly all of the mines were closed. In 1933, the E. T. Fisher
Company built and operated a dredge on the streams
near town. In a ten-mile stretch, they took out seven hundred thousand dollars in gold. The massive "traveling mill"
was mounted on rails. It pulled itself forward as it chewed
at the gravel banks of Rock Creek. Two men could handle
the operation. One controlled the dredge, the second took
care of the two-story gold washer, oiling bearings and

This gold washer received many thousands of dollars' worth of gold from the sands and gravels of Rock Creek. Tracks were lifted from the rear and laid down in front as the operation eroded its way along a dozen miles of stream bed.

watching for nuggets. Nuggets over an inch in diameter were generally carried out with the waste gravel! A sharp eye and quick hand were necessary at the final sorting table, lest a small fortune be returned to the water.

The Carpenter Hotel was the only business operating in Atlantic City in 1950, but it operated with a flair. An overnight cabin, complete with brass bedstead and "saggy" springs, was one dollar. Meals were fifty cents, with an added fee of twenty-five cents if you failed to carry your dishes to the kitchen.

If you drive twenty-seven miles south of Lander on Wyo-

Interior of the Rose Mine, showing cleats nailed to the beams of the head frame, forming a rough ladder. The vertical shaft is located in the center of the picture. The vein was rich but short-lived.

ming Highway 28, then take a good gravel road left for a bit less than five miles you will reach the remains of this famous Wyoming ghost town. There is much left to see. On a hill at the north edge of town is the church, well preserved and beautiful, richly deserving its title of National Shrine. At the bend in the street is the old rock building of McAuley's. The upper story is gone, due to a minor earthquake some years ago. The lower floor is intact, and the building has been reroofed by its present owner, Tom Hyde. It is now called "Hyde's Hall," and to make sure there is no dispute regarding ownership, the building has been branded—twice—with a bold TH. The old livery is

"Modern-day" prospectors abandoned this gasoline-powered gold washer in the thirties. Built like a cement mixer, it operated as a rotary sluice box. Note the overlength axle.

standing, leaning more every year. The candy kitchen built in 1902 is still in good shape, but sadly empty of sweets. A dozen well-preserved homes still dot the hillside. Giessler's Store is open again, under the management of Mr. and Mrs. Moerer.

The hotel is operating too, but meals are five dollars now, and by reservation only.

Within a few miles of town are a number of mines, still intact, awaiting possible reactivation. Of note are the Diana, Garfield, Caribou, Tabor, King Solomon, and the Rose mines.

A few miles downstream from town on Rock Creek is the nearly intact gold washer, no longer sorting its gravels, and making its poor decisions regarding nuggets.

Topographic maps of this area are a must for complete exploration. *The Miner's Delight, Atlantic City, Louis Lake, and South Pass City, Wyoming, 7½ minute topographic maps* cover the area in detail.

The Eclipse Hotel, a dining hall, and the express office. The latter is braced, and is next on the list of buildings to be restored.

SOUTH PASS CITY, WYOMING

Gold seekers settled on Willow Creek in 1867. The camp soon became a town, and the town became the largest in the state. Named South Pass City, it grew quickly. Within eighteen months, its population exceeded two thousand. What should have been a curly-haired, short-tempered saloon town, became, instead, a family community. Those miners with wives and children, seeking a safe home, chose this town rather than Atlantic City, located five miles east. The women were quick to organize and preserve this precious quality. Some say organization was hastened by the several long meetings held during the Indian raids. Hostiles frequently threatened the town, driving off the stock and stealing whatever was left unguarded. During the raids, the

The strongly barred jail had cells along the rear wall. The building to the right was originally the Esther Morris Hat shop. Later, it was converted to a saloon.

women and children were locked in a cavelike recess behind the wine celler owned by a local merchant. The celler was protected by a stout iron door. Many a decision was made in the darkness of this hideaway.

Under less frightening circumstances, the women organized a club, held numerous meetings, and discussed women's rights. Mrs. Esther Hobart Morris, who came to South Pass in 1869, was a strong advocate of women's right to vote. That year, encouraged by the women club members, Mr. William Bright drafted a bill giving equal suffrage to women. The bill was introduced and passed! Shortly after, Mrs. Esther Hobart Morris was appointed justice of the peace. Many heated cases were accorded a decision by the good lady. None of them was overruled by a higher court.

*Now a museum, this well-built log structure was originally a
general store operated by Smith and Sherlock.*

However quiet, South Pass City was still a mining town.
Its Main Street was crowded with false-fronted buildings,
nearly every other one a saloon. Main Street was nearly a
half mile long. The town had the first bank in the area, a
well-organized school system, a newspaper, and a regular
stage service.

The Carissa Lode, the richest deposit in the area, poured
forth its wealth, and the town prospered. A few other mines
in the area were producing, like the Franklin, the Shields,
and the Jim Crow Hoosier Boy, but the Carissa was the big
one, and when its vein pinched out, the life of the town began
to flicker. By 1880, South Pass City was nearly deserted.
Many buildings were moved away, but each of those remaining has a story to tell.

The jail is still in fine shape, the cell doors swinging free-

South Pass City lies quietly under the watchful eye of the famous Carissa Mine. Main Street, extending from left to right, was over two thousand feet long.

ly. It is clearly evident why it was later called "the cooler." Even the town dog likes to sleep here on hot summer days. Next to the jail is the old hat shop, later converted to a saloon. The Smith Sherlock store has been recently converted to a museum. The town is undergoing a continuing process of restoration.

South Pass City is a quiet place in the summer, and completely deserted each winter. A lonely graveyard overlooks the town from the south. On the northern hill, the Carissa Mine patiently waits reactivation. A single caretaker watches over the massive investment. Perhaps a new and cheaper way to extract the gold will be found, and the giant will stir to life again.

Emigrants came over the summit of South Pass, shown in the background. The town was often mired so deeply in mud that the wagon trains camped a mile to the south on high ground. The two-story livery is on the left.

PACIFIC SPRINGS, WYOMING

Once called the "Old Halter and Flick Ranch," this unique town, founded in 1853, is referred to by old-timers as the "muddiest damned spot on the Lander-Rawlins Stage Road."

It is indeed muddy! Situated on a swampy flat at an elevation of 7,200 feet, the waters of the Pacific Springs meander about, sending fingers of water in all directions. During the spring rains, the main street was unsafe, and it was the only street in town.

This relatively unknown site can be reached easily by driving to the highway from South Pass City, then heading southwest for twelve and a half miles. Visible on the left, about one mile distant, is the cluster of buildings called Pacific Springs. A good dirt road leads across the railroad

Interior of the livery that once held fresh horses for the stage and Pony Express. Also called the Halter and Flick Ranch, the town is now completely deserted.

tracks, circles to the right and enters town. The *Pacific Springs and Anderson Ridge, Wyoming, 7½ minute topographic maps* locate the site.

Although eight of its buildings have been moved away, five structures remain. The romance of a very old and well-deserted town is still present. A two-story barn, or livery, is on the north side, complete with eight double stalls. It was originally used to provide shelter for relay horses used by the stage and Pony Express lines.

The old Pacific Springs store is intact, but does not display the expected false front. The town was built before such refinements became commonplace. The store has long since been converted to a storage house for a nearby ranch.

Used for storage by local ranchers, this building was at various times a store, a residence, and a post office.

Two residences and a log soddy complete the remains of what was once the celebration spot on the Oregon Trail.

This site marked the first camping spot for emigrants after crossing South Pass. The pass is only seventy-four hundred feet high, but subject to severe storms in early and late summer. Many travelers celebrated the evening of the crossing, only to wake up and face the double hazard of a hangover—and three miles of mud.

By 1918, the town had faded to just a post office named Pacific. Recently a railroad has constructed a line that passes close by the edge of town. It brought no hope of revival. The tracks are a recent development of the U.S. Steel Corporation. The trains on this line haul concentrated iron ore from a mine and mill north of Atlantic City to the Union Pacific line to the south. The train is automated and needs no crew. This would indicate that special precautions are appropriate. Should your vehicle stall or high-center at the crossing, don't attempt to flag this train down. Just step back and resign yourself to one dandy collision!

*"Hard Rock Sam" Vjestic worked in almost every mine in the area.
Born in 1893, he arrived in Wyoming barely in time to
be a part of the last mining effort.*

MINERS DELIGHT, WYOMING

In the existing literature concerning ghost towns in Wyoming, only a sketch of Miners Delight is shown. This sketch portrays a row of miners' cabins, and the caption states that they were nearly overgrown with brush. It seems that most writers and historians since that time figured the town was gone. If a sketch was the only means of demonstrating its existence, then, it was reasoned, there could be little of the town remaining. It was a ridiculous assumption and it gave "Hard Rock Sam" Vjestic the best laugh he'd had in years. "Why—dere's lots old cabins dere, and the mine even got da hoist wheel still dere. And lots old cabins down da line in town—Yah—dots a good one—all gone is it? Yah—Yah!"

Sam Vjestic is a long-time resident of the Sweetwater Mining District. This old-timer was born in 1893 and worked most of his life in the nearby mines. He has a great memory, and an even greater sense of humor. "Why, I remember da last time I got mad. Yah—vas in 1938—too

Looking west down the main street of Miners Delight. Traffic is light.
The cabin in the center was updated with metal roofing,
but the insulating layer of dirt was retained.

much Kentucky Club and Muscatel—but I pass out before
I do much damage."

Sam was happy to give directions to Miners Delight, and
volunteered to go along on some future trips.

From Atlantic City, a gravel road leads back toward
Lander. In a bit over two miles, a dirt road branches to the
right, or east. Immediately a small stream is forded. In
another one and one-half miles you will pass the Gold Dollar
Mine, and a little more than a mile beyond is the Miners
Delight cemetery. A left turn, and another quarter of a
mile puts you on the main east-west street of Miners Delight. The same topographic maps used for Atlantic City
will also show these sites.

There are indeed a dozen structures still standing, some
of them at acute angles with the vertical, others in nearly
horizontal repose. A few of the cabins show signs of recent occupancy. Some ingenious person found a way of
making the interior brighter in one of the log structures.

The fanciest house in town. Note the hand-squared log construction, and the old wagon bows leaning by the door.

White surfaces would reflect much of the light from the rather dim kerosene lamps, but it is nearly impossible to paint the inside of a log building. The solution? Just tack up some white cloth—on the ceiling, the walls—even on the inside of the door. The cloth now hangs in tatters, and it is rather spooky walking through these veils of dusty white, especially when a pack rat scratches out a frantic retreat!

Martha Jane Canary, better known as "Calamity Jane," was likely the town's most infamous character. Orphaned at an early age, some kindly folk adopted her. Calamity and her new parents moved to Miners Delight during its first year of existence. Shortly thereafter, a "wordly lady" from the East talked Martha (Calamity) Jane into visiting New York. A year later Martha was back, thoroughly educated, and in business for herself. The ladies of Miners Delight

A custom stamp mill, probably used also as a smithy and repair shop.
It is located between the town of Miners Delight and the mine.

were shocked at her activities, and amazed that "one so young could fall so quickly." The town's women heaved a sigh of relief when it was learned that Jane had moved to Atlantic City and was operating the dance hall above Mc-Auley's Store.

History has converted this well-known "sporting girl" from a "tenderloin lady" to a heroine of high morals, and the folk living in the area are now proud to state that "Miners Delight was Calamity's home town."

At the west edge of town are the remains of what appears to be a smithy, or a "one stamp" mill. Perhaps it served both functions. All the metal work is gone, but the strong overhead timbers imply a hoisting function, either for equipment repairs or for a heavy stamper. One can speculate that samples from the mine were brought here for quick analysis.

Gallows frame of the famous Miners Delight Mine, richest property in the entire Sweetwater drainage. A million in gold was taken from this hole in just a few short years.

One of a row of miners' cabins just opposite the mine shaft. The willows and aspens that hide these cabins are responsible for the town being reported as "leveled to the ground."

Located in Spring Gulch, the town was founded by Herman Nickerson and friends in 1867. They had located some "color" in the gulch, and promptly laid out a town. Originally called Hamilton City, the name was changed when the upstart Miners Delight Mine just west of town proved to be the "biggest pay" in the whole area. The rich vein contained free gold in quartz and the gold was abundant. A mule-drawn arrastra or drag stone mill was soon crushing the quartz, and men were were hired to pan out the gold. Three hundred thousand dollars' worth of gold was taken out the first year! The shaft was one hundred and fifty feet deep, and the vein varied from three to fourteen feet thick. The ore ran to one thousand dollars per ton. Since 1874, the mine has been dewatered and reworked seven times. The last time was in 1927. The head frame is standing yet, and some tracks are still there, but the rolling stock has been removed, and all is now quiet.

Near the mine, buried in deep brush, is the long row of

The Monte Carlo Mine, one mile northwest of Miners Delight. An unsuccessful attempt was made here to hit the main gold-bearing ledge originally tapped by the Miners Delight shaft.

miners' shacks. The corner of one shack peeks out far enough to be photographed. These nearly invisible cabins, and a few strokes of charcoal on paper, are responsible for the town's present undisturbed quality. The belief that little was left to see gave Miners Delight a chance to survive intact.

THE DUNCAN, WYOMING

From Atlantic City, an excellent gravel road winds steeply up Mill Hill, levels off and heads southeast. At the crest, one mile south of town, a dirt road branches to the right. Traveling this road westward, the Mary Ellen Mine comes quickly into view. Then, within a mile of the turnoff, "The Duncan"

First powered by steam, then converted to electricity, The Duncan
Mine had everything it took to "make a million"—except rich
ore. Today, shuttered and locked, The Duncan
awaits a rise in the price of gold.

Sprawling over the hillside, The Duncan mill accepted raw ore at the top, crushed it, and passed it downhill from process to process. Even with the best of equipment, the effort failed to make a profit.

becomes visible. Both mines are on the right side of the road, and are on the *Atlantic City, Wyoming, 7½ minute topographic* map.

The first rich strike was made here in 1911. In three years, forty thousand dollars' worth of ore was removed. During those three years, fifteen hundred feet of underground tunnels and shafts were completed, and a Nissen stamp mill and amalgamator were installed. The outfit was capable of extracting 60 percent of the gold. In 1914 the operation ran into financial trouble, and the mine closed down.

Thirty-two years later, new owners gave it another try. A new ball mill, classifier, and several agitator tanks were obtained. Eight flotation cells and a concentrator, or shaker table, were installed. Just twelve tons of ore were processed that year, valued at a total of about two thousand dollars. In 1956, the mine underwent another hopeful spurt of activity, with three thousand tons shipped at about twelve

Two-story dormitory for the "hard rockers." It was hoped that the mill would operate the year round, twenty-four hours a day. The mine head is immediately behind.

The dormitory is to the right, the mine-head structures to the left. Family residences are in the foreground.. Not shown are the mill and repair shops.

dollars per ton. During its busiest years, "The Duncan" rivaled in size the towns of Atlantic City and Miners Delight. Several dozen cabins, a small store, and a two-story dormitory occupied most of the level area at the top of the hill. The mine buildings cover the hillside for hundreds of feet, ending in another smattering of buildings.

Now everything is shuttered and locked, awaiting a rise in the price of gold. The houses are vacant. The dormitory, with its outside stairs, is quiet, and heavy boots no longer threaten the quick nap of the man on the "off shift."

A rusty, well-worn ore car rests impatiently at the crossing. After loading, the car was pushed to the left and its contents dumped over the mill hopper. If the car was loaded with waste rock, it was sent out on the alternate tracks leading to the waste dump.

The old store at Lewiston will probably not stand up for many more years. Gutted, and in the process of collapsing, it still shows evidence of past glories.

LEWISTON, WYOMING

"Lewiston? What Lewiston? In Wyoming? Never heard of it!" But the entire population of Atlantic City knew about the town—all four of them. In fact, one of them used to live there! Good old Sam Vjestic—and he promptly volunteered to ride along on a visit to the townsite. Was there anything left, as the map indicated—or was it all gone, as some historians claimed?

"Vell, dere's a store, und a liffery, und some mines dere," volunteered Sam.

We drove south out of Atlantic City, up Mill Hill, past The Duncan turnoff, and headed east on a good gravel road. About eight miles out of town, Sam called for an abrupt turn to the right. Here on the banks of Rock Creek, rested a monument—a bronze slab cemented to a mound of rock. Inscribed on the plaque is a story of nearly unequaled tragedy.

WILLIE'S HANDCART COMPANY

Captain James C. Willie's Handcart Company of Mormon Emigrants on the way to Utah, greatly exhausted by the deep snows of an early winter and suffering from lack of food and clothing had assembled here for reorganization by relief parties from Utah about the end of October 1865. Thirteen persons were frozen to death during a single night and were buried here in one grave. Two others died the next day and were buried nearby. Of the company of 404 persons 77 perished before help arrived. The survivors reached Salt Lake November 9 1856.

The South Pass was indeed treacherous! It was quite clear now why Pacific Springs was called "Celebration City."

About four miles farther east we took a fork to the left, forded Strawberry Creek, and drove into the town of Lewiston. The *Radium Springs, Wyoming, 7½ minute topographic* map shows most of the important sites in fine detail. Part of this map is reproduced in the Introduction.

Lewiston isn't very big—just two buildings with a street between. On the left was the old store, false front and all.

On the right was the livery, its interlocking logs holding it firmly plumb with the world. The store had five rooms and showed signs of frequent haphazard expansion. Its sod roof, supported by large split logs, had collapsed in a number of places. The most recent occupants had been sheep and cattle. Cattle enjoy scratching themselves by rubbing against door jambs, and once the door is knocked off, a building comes down quickly. The Lewiston Store will not stand for long.

The livery looked like it would photograph best from the rear. The view through the finder showed that I was a bit too close. I backed up a few feet and stopped. Not far enough yet. I backed up a few feet more, focused the camera, and took the picture. Behind me I could hear the clatter of pebbles falling, bouncing, and fading into faint echoes. I had backed up to the very brink of a deep vertical mine shaft. I circled back another dozen feet and photographed the livery, with the site of my stupidity in the foreground.

This town once had more than twenty-five buildings, including four saloons, which is a pretty low "sin percentage," as mining towns go. It had several mines right in town, the most famous of which was the Bullion Shaft. Founded in 1879, Lewiston was the center of the "new discovery." Much salting and selling was carried out. Each "sucker" salted in turn, and made money selling to the next buyer.

One-half mile south of town are the remains of the Hidden

A deep shaft behind the livery may trap the unwary visitor. The left part of the building was used as a residence at one time. The covered rear porch has collapsed.

*Shaft house and smithy of the Hidden Hand Mine. Sam Vjestic views
a sample from the diggings. Sam worked underground
at this mine for a number of years.*

Hand Mine. Forty feet away is the Iron Duke Shaft. I
speculated that two shafts this close had to lead to the same
vein. Sam Vjestic added "dey haf to lead to a good fight
when da tunnels meet, too!" Sam knew what he was talking
about, for he spent several years hogging out the rock in order to form those shafts!

One-half mile to the north is the Good Hope Mine. This
building is in a most artistic state of disrepair. As its lower
side walls collapsed, its stout inner structure guided the outer portions downward to rest sedately, with a dignified list
to port. Like a crippled queen of the oceans, it rides the
windswept plains, valiantly resisting the inevitable.

A family of wildcats lives in the old relic. They have been
seen standing on the peak of the gallows frame, and no
doubt found some crevice suitable for a den. More hazardous than the wildcats is the horizontal tunnel running
out from the building. In places the tunnel is within a foot
or two of the surface. Your weight might collapse it. Your
car most certainly would break through.

The shaft house of the Good Hope Mine seems to lean back in resignation, contemplating the onset of winter.

It had been a long day, and we were tired. The return trip was hot, dry, and dusty. As we neared Atlantic City, I suggested we stop for a cooling drink at Giessler's Saloon. Sam's eyes lit up. "Yah, I haf a coke." Realizing a coke might be pretty tame stuff for a tough old miner like Sam, I suggested something with more substance. "Naw," replied Sam. "I swear off dat hard stuff ever since I get mad back in 'thirty-eight."

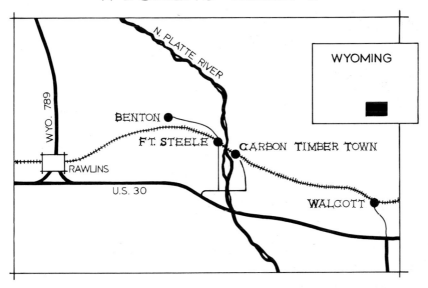

FORT STEELE, WYOMING

THE UNION PACIFIC was driving its rails west. The mountains of eastern Wyoming had been breached. West of Laramie, the land leveled out to plains and high desert, permitting more rapid progress, but the flat land was Indian land, and the Indians resented the intrusion.

Fort Steele was established in 1868 to protect the Overland Stage Line and the Union Pacific railroad. The presence of four companies (about three hundred men) encouraged construction and safeguarded travelers.

Located at the Overland Trail crossing of the North Platte River, the fort was ideally placed to carry out its protective function. Within forty-eight hours of the arrival of troops, ruffians and crooks had set up shop a half mile to the south at a place called Brownsville. A typical railhead town, stores, eating houses, saloons, and gambling joints fronted the street, and sporting houses were placed behind. The population of Brownsville reached fifteen hundred within a week. The Army, claiming it was a bad influence, kicked the town off Government land. Brownsville, only weeks old, promptly moved three miles to the western boundary of the fort, and renamed itself "Benton." It became "the one bad town on the U.P."

Enlisted men's barracks, built in 1868, were later converted to the Fort Steele General Store, then to sheep company storage sheds. Note sign: "Water Your Auto Here."

Fort Steele was built around a small parade ground. There was no stockade, and none was needed. Records indicate that the soldiers never met the enemy in battle. Gravel walks surrounded the parade ground and fronted the buildings. The west side was "Officers' Row." Four two-story buildings each housed about twenty officers. The central building was the residence of the commanding officer. On the east side were enlisted men's barracks, laundries, and a sawmill. The railroad passed by the south side, separating the fort from the sutler's post and saloon.

In 1886 the fort was abandoned. Eight years later the property was purchased by the Cosgriff Brothers for one hundred dollars. They converted the buildings to stores and residences. One of the officers' quarters became a hotel and the powder house a granary. The saloon remained a saloon.

*Rear view of the only remaining officers' quarters. Note the hallways
leading to "indoor outhouses." Side areas of the halls were
used as tack rooms, a storage place for saddles,
boots, guns, and other gear.*

Later, fire destroyed much of the town. The remaining
buildings became the property of the Leo Sheep Company.

The site of Fort Fred Steele (later the town of Fort
Steele), is reached by traveling twelve miles east of Rawlins on Highway 80, then north two miles along the west
bank of the Platte River. The fort, its parade ground still
prominent, is just across the Union Pacific tracks. The *Walcott, Wyoming, 15 minute topographic* map is of notable
help. Dated 1912, it shows much of the fort as it used to
be. Many of the buildings indicated on the map are now
merely foundations or depressions in the ground. Much of
the old glory has faded—the enlisted men's barracks are
filled with barbed wire, salt, wool, and old sheep hides. The
gable end of the building nearest the railroad tracks carries
evidence of a number of uses. Several signs have been lettered on its front. The most prominent and probably the
last: "Ft. Steele General Store." Below is a sign: "WATER
YOUR AUTO HERE."

This badly abused portion of the old barracks shows the log construction covered with spacers and lap siding. The inside was similarly treated.

Thick grout walls survive well in the dry Wyoming climate. This building was once the home of acting Governor Chatterton.

One building stands on Officer's Row. In remarkably good shape, it is like two houses glued together—each the exact mirror image of the other. A single partition separates the two stairways as they lead side by side to the bedrooms on the upper level. Behind the building are two "hallway" extensions. Each leads to its own indoor outhouse. The "privilege of rank" was particularly appreciated on frosty mornings, but the price paid was the ever-present odor. Perhaps a better term would be "rank privilege." As the cesspools filled, the hallways were extended to reach freshly dug pits. Some old forts had hallways up to sixty feet long. The life of Fort Steele was short—and so were its outhouse extensions.

On the hill, just southwest of the old "fort become town," are the remains of acting Governor Chatterton's home. The poured walls are eighteen inches thick. Old-fashioned concrete, called grout, was made with burned lime and unwashed gravel. The joists and rafters were poured in place.

The Richard's Toll Bridge, located near Fort Steele, was

The powder house is now used as a granary. Small holes at the top permitted the air to circulate, keeping the powder dry.

in operation during the years of emigration. Built for $5,000, it took in $40,000 in toll the first season. Fording the North Platte River was often dangerous. The graveyard just south of the fort gives evidence of such hazard on several headstones.

Glassing the riverbank, trying to spot the old bridge abutments, I noticed a timbered trestle, perhaps the remnant of a bridge approach. The caretaker at the nearby waterworks (for the town of Rawlins) supplied some brief answers.

"No, it's not a bridge." Pressed for more information, the caretaker added, "Bunch of buildings over there. We call it "Timber Town."

That was exciting news. My topographic map showed some buildings there, but I had been given to understand they had all been demolished. The remains of the old town of Benton were nearby, and on the Fort Steele side of the river. A hurried visit to that site, then the "bunch of buildings" would have to be looked into carefully.

BENTON, WYOMING

Called "Wild Town" and "Outlaw Town," preceded generally by unprintable expletives, Benton was likely the wildest town ever to exist in Wyoming. There is nothing left of the town, just one hell of a story and millions of broken bits of glass from bottles emptied and thrown.

Benton was the illegitimate child of the Union Pacific. Three miles west of the fort, it was beyond military control, yet close enough to attract the fort's several hundred troopers. It was the tent town railhead at the seven hundred mile marker, measured west from Omaha. It was born on July 1, 1868, when the Army kicked the town of Brownsville off their reservation. It died in September, 1868, at the age of three months. But what a summer! One hundred people were killed in three wild months.

There were no trees, the ground was bare, and the alkali was six inches deep underfoot. Stolen locomotive headlights illuminated seductively decorated billboards. The North Star Saloon and the Desert Hotel were prominent institutions of doubtful character. Other business houses carried signs bordered in red, and needed no explanation, for the street was their front parlor. Twenty-three saloons dispensed beer, bitters, and bourbon. Five dance halls offered the same fare—but with added attractions.

Three thousand people lived in Benton, and on weekends it neared five thousand. Lots sold for one thousand dollars, and the main street was sold out. Water was scarce. Hauled from the Platte River, it sold for a dollar a barrel. One former resident recorded an "irregularity" concerning the delivery of water. A mule skinner had just hauled the water in on a skid. Being thirsty, he adjourned to the nearest bar and tipped a few. He came out in time to see the mules backed up to the first row of barrels, one animal responding to the call of nature. He sold the barrel and explained, "Hell, it was so damned muddy you couldn't see the bottom anyway."

CARBON TIMBER TOWN, WYOMING

It was time to investigate "Timber Town" across the river. Returning through Fort Steele, I stopped at the powder house and once again glassed the far bank. A few roofs were visible, but no entering road was evident. I returned

*The main street of Carbon Timber Town—a classic among "unknown"
ghost towns—is overgrown from long disuse.*

south, two miles to the rest area adjacent to Interstate 80.
The old highway bridge gave me access to the east bank.
Shortly, a gravel road turned northward, but dead-ended
in a gravel pit. A bit farther, a second road branched to the
north. A mile north on this road, and I could see a row of
wooden structures. The farthest building was large and
carried a high false front. There was no road into town.
Bridges over the backwaters and gullies had broken down

*Sign on the store front reads: "Carbon Timber Co., Store
Dept." Inside is an old walk-in ice cooler.*

with time. I walked the few hundred yards into town. Feel-
ing like a character out of an old Western, I strolled down
the main street. It was grass-grown and long untraveled.
The left side was lined with "look alike" hip-roofed company houses. A large false-fronted building at the end of
the row of houses was obviously a store. The printing on
the front was barely legible. After some study, I could make
out:

"CARBON TIMBER CO. STORE DEPT."

The window display portion of the store front was knocked
out. I stepped inside to investigate the interior. It was
spacious and completely empty. The floor was flexible and
had broken through in places. Toward the rear was a vault-
like room with a thick wooden tapered door. Above it was
another room with a small access door. Sawdust gave the

This old-fashioned dug well is rock-lined and still full of water, although unused for nearly forty years.

answer. Ice had been thrown in the upper compartment. The lower room was obviously a walk-in cooler. Behind the store was an old-fashioned dug well. Indeed, there were wells behind every building. Each well was lined with rock, and some had wooden casings extending above ground. One well was complete with overhead framework. The pulley wheel, rope, and bucket were gone, but the well still had water close to ground level.

Railroad tracks seemed to branch everywhere. Each spur led to another structure, and each structure presented a new mystery. One old cabin located near the junction of several spurs had a walkway between the tracks and the front door. Perhaps the head engineer lived here and parked his train in front of the house each night. I found out later that this speculation was correct. Also, that the engineer had signals arranged with his wife: three short toots meant he would pass by the house shortly, and to please have coffee ready to hand up to the cab.

Above town (upstream), the river branches to form two channels. The right-hand part is wide and slow. Along this channel, just before it rejoins the main stream, are a number of odd remnants. Attached to the bank by cable is a long, free-floating dock or pier, constructed of hundreds of railroad ties, each pointed toward midstream. At the up- and downstream ends are two small open-ended sheds. A ramp leads steeply upward from each shed. The ramps end abruptly about eleven feet above, and directly over an old railroad spur. Each ramp has two grooves, up which railroad ties or logs were moved by some means or other. Centrally located, and two stories high, a third shed houses a concrete foundation and large belt-type wheel. An axle extends from this wheel to both extremes, and terminates with two more wheels that line up with the inclined ramps. This would indicate that endless belts were used to send a "never-ending" string of ties from stream level to the top of the ramp. From there they were stacked on or loaded into railroad cars and transported to the railhead. Logically, then, the ties were originally floated downriver from the high forests of the Snowy Range. As they reached the division in the stream, they were shunted to the slower bypass, then caught and sent up the loading ramps.

There must have been a number of boats used in this operation. It would provide considerable satisfaction if I could find the remains of such a craft. I worked my way

A double-barreled tie "snake-out." Brush has overgrown the river's channel immediately behind the shack. Endless belts once hoisted ties to railroad cars for transport to railhead.

downriver, searching the banks for a boat, boat ramp, or, hopefully, a boathouse. I immediately found another ramp, but it was similar to the tie snake-out ramps. This one was "single-barrelled," but led to a long trestle, the one I had originally observed from across the river. The trestle, actually a loading platform, was about one thousand feet long, and there were tracks alongside for most of its length. Down the center of the fourteen-foot-high, eighteen-foot-wide structure, was provision for a very long, endless belt. Engine foundations of concrete stood at the landward end of the trestle. This ramp and platform were probably used for loading logs, and it appeared that thirty cars could be loaded at one time.

Still there was no sign of a boat! Downstream a short distance were another ramp and trestle, similar to the "log loader." Nearby were grout abutments in which metal hooks had been imbedded. Remnants of cables lay about. The booms that once spanned the river must have been anchored here. There seemed to be little doubt now as to the function of this old town. Still, it would be nice if I could find a boat.

Shortly downstream, next to the railroad bridge, were the extensive jackstraw ruins of an old sawmill. The machinery was gone, but the ramps, tracks, skids, axle bearings, and engine foundations clearly spelled "sawmill." There was no sawdust! Yet it had to be a sawmill. I was still considering the sawdust problem when I stumbled upon the boat!

It was a stout old craft, sixteen feet long, five and a half feet wide, and fastened throughout with bolts. Round-bottomed and squared off at bow and stern, the lap-streaked craft still retained its original contours. There were no oarlocks or seats, and no indication that the craft was ever equipped with such refinements.

Not all facets of Carbon Timber Town were easily deciphered. There was a large brick building between the store and the sawmill. It looked like a powerhouse, a blacksmith's shop, and a livery all rolled into one. Several more buildings defied explanation. There were many questions yet unanswered. I inquired at the local County Museum and at the State Archives. Limited information concerning the company town was available from these sources. While photographing other ghost towns in the area, I had the chance to visit with a number of people, some of them old-timers. Questions about Carbon Timber Town were most often answered with blank stares. One old gent insisted there was no such town or he would have known about it. The situation was difficult. The "no" answers were followed by short challenges concerning my sanity, or long questions concerning this mysterious town. Another ghost town in the area, named "Carbon," added to the confusion.

Several weeks later I was gathering information on the

A long trestle with equally long endless belt carried logs from the river, permitting thirty flatcars to be loaded simultaneously.

old railroad town of Hanna, Wyoming. Mr. Lionel Love was telling me of his boyhood in this coal-mining area. Lionel and his wife Irene impressed me with their accurate recall. I asked if he was acquainted with Fort Steele.

"Yeah, used to work across the river at Carbon Timber Town."

Several hours later I had asked all of my pent-up questions and heard some interesting stories about the old tie drives.

According to Mr. Love, the tie ramps were much as I had speculated, except that there were three double snake-outs. Thirty-six men could load fourteen thousand ties in nine hours. Ties flattened on just two sides were common until 1929. After then, logs were sent to Laramie for "squaring by saw."

The hole in the store front? Boats used in the tie drives were stored there. Someone removed them the easy way. Between the store and the first house was an old foundation with a brick vault still intact. Lionel said this was the site

Ruins of an old sawmill. The brick and grout
powerhouse stands at the left.

of the company office. He used to stand in line there to pick
up his pay. Later it became a cookhouse. The boat by the
sawmill was used for "running" the boom. Generally, six
men kneeled and paddled, three to a side. The sawdust?
Some was used for ice storage. The "loners" or bachelors
who lived in the shacks nearby took some. It kept them
warm all winter. The brick building was once a powerhouse
—really just a big boiler—steam pipes led to steam engines
at each of the loading ramps. Later the building was converted to a box factory.

The first ties came down the North Platte River shortly
after the establishment of Fort Steele in 1868. During a
drive, the ties strung out for twenty miles. With 500,000
ties, it required dozens of men to refloat those that stuck
or grounded. It took two months to chase them from the
mountains to the railroad. The drives were conducted almost yearly up to 1931. Saratoga was the halfway point.
Here the ties were forgotten while the men got down to
serious drinking. A week later—sometimes longer—the

The old boom-tending boat is sixteen feet long and stoutly bolted together. Metal patches cover damaged spots caused by minor collisions with logs.

cleanup operation continued. Most of the men rode down the stream on two ties, taking care to keep them tightly together, lest a king-size pinch result. It was a cold, wet job —dangerous for those who couldn't swim! Wet all day and dry all night for a month at a time was carrying on a courtship with pneumonia. Some hacks slept wet, never changed clothes or attempted to dry their blankets. Fewer colds resulted. Those who did catch cold were put in the duffel or cook boat and given dry but mundane chores.

Squeak heel was a malady peculiar to the tie-hack. Constant exposure to cool (not ice-cold) water, caused the Achilles tendon to contract. When this tendon tightened up, the only recourse was to walk on tiptoe. Exercise and massage generally relaxed the calf muscle, permitting normal use within a few days.

Some hacks were tie jam experts. They knew where to put the dynamite to break the jam loose. It was common to dive under the jam to locate the "key tie," then to dive

Crumbling brick and a tired pulley wheel mark the remains of a powerhouse later converted to a box factory.

again and plant the charge. Gunard Ingermason was a daredevil. Once, when he dove under the jam and found the key tie, he merely braced his feet and pulled. The ties tumbled all about Gunard as he swam under the water in front of the loosened ties. He surfaced downstream and walked back to find a search going on for the "body of poor old Gunard."

The Walcott map shows both the fort on the west side of the river, and "Carbon Timber Town" on the east bank. The entire complex is labeled Fort Steele. Originally, the fort occupied a large square area, six miles on a side. Anything within the boundary was by definition "Fort Steele." Later, when the fort was abandoned, the two communities took on separate identities. The fort proper became a country store and gas station under the name of Fort Steele. "East Fort Steele," became better known as a company timber operation. Which name to use? The answer is obvious. The neighbor across the river, the old tie hack, and the sign above the store agree—"Carbon Timber Town."

WALCOTT, WYOMING

From 1890 to 1910, Walcott was the busiest railroad loading point between Omaha, Nebraska, and Ogden, Utah. Mining machinery and building materials were hauled in— copper ore and cattle were sent out. There was a hotel on the north side of the tracks next to the depot. Two livery stables and a number of stores and saloons flanked the dirt road entering from the south. Several hundred people lived here during the mining boom, but as time passed, unfortunate things happened to Walcott. The copper mines and smelters of Encampment, to the south, went broke. A highway was built, bypassing the town. As a final insult, the Union Pacific depot was removed in 1940.

There are two Walcotts now. The "new highway Walcott" is seven miles east of the Fort Steele turnoff. The "railroad Walcott" is one mile north. Both are shown on the *Walcott, Wyoming, 15 minute topographic map*. There are two fascinating points of interest at the site of the railroad town. One is the old saloon, and the other is its caretaker, Slim Parkko.

The saloon has a sign on its false front that is a work of art. In fancy scroll and block letters it states:

The "Glub &aloon" (with a scrolly G and an S turned backward) stands on the south side—the wrong side—of the tracks, but on the main freight route to the copper mines.

THE GLUB &ALOON
JOHN H. LEWIS

The "S" is backwards in "saloon," but correct in "Lewis!" Perhaps it was intended to be the "Club Saloon," with a scrolly "C," but it looked like a "G"—and "Glub" had an appropriate sound—so "Glub" it became. If it brought in customers, Proprietor Lewis wasn't about to change it.

An old rusted tin sign on the saloon states:

Cornone Cigar Company's
DRY CLIMATE
A Cigar Built for the Altitude

Across the tracks are a number of the old cabins of Walcott. Now they are used by the Vivian Sheep Company. Old wooden wagon wheels lean everywhere. Removed from

Some of the old cabins at Walcott are serving as storage areas for a sheep company. Rubber tires are replacing the oak spoke wheels that once cut narrow ruts in the town's streets.

sheep wagons, they have been replaced with rubber-tired wheels.

On my way out of town I stopped to visit with one of the few surviving residents of Walcott. He lives in a well-kept little house just behind the "Glub Saloon." A veteran sheepman, he introduced himself as "Slim" Parkko, and—like the saloon—he was most descriptively named.

"Does that sign really read the 'Glub' Saloon," I asked. Slim replied, "Yup."

"How many people are living here now?"

Slim looked across the tracks. "Them two and just me."

"Is that little building up on the hill an old water tank?"

"Yup," said Slim, looking a little tired from such continued effort.

As I left town, I looked back at the meager remains of this once busy freighting junction. The town was well suited to its leading citizen. Walcott—like Slim's conversation—was "real sparse."

PART V
MONTANA

MONTANA AREA 1

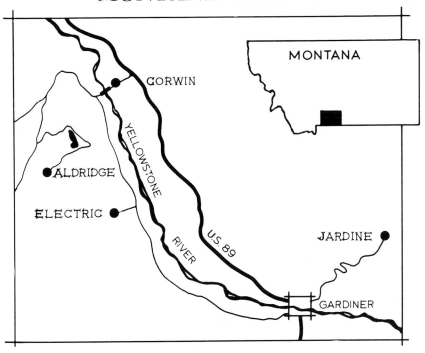

JARDINE, MONTANA

FROM GARDNER, at the north edge of Yellowstone Park, it is six miles by gravel road to the town of Jardine. These are six of Montana's prettiest miles. The road angles up the north side of Yellowstone Canyon, crosses Eagle Creek, and immediately drops over a rise, bringing the green valley of Bear Creek into view.

Two and a half miles ahead lies the old mining town of Jardine, but here, beside the road, is a scene of unusual beauty. A small pond, its deep waters lightly rippled by the breeze, nestles between the road and a curve of protecting trees. Toward the far shore, a weathered shack stands in deep water. A gangplank offers access, and inside are rusted control wheels, their axles extending deep below the water's surface.

The lake seems too peaceful—too natural—to be man-made, but it is in fact the headwater pond of a hydroelectric plant. A three-mile ditch contours its way from the upper reaches of Bear Creek, bringing water gently to this point.

A picturesque head-gate shack controls the water flow leading downhill to a double waterwheel. Power developed here was converted to electricity and used to drive the mills of Jardine.

The waters of Bear Creek tumble past the remains of the old Revenue Mill. Most of the ore processed here was mined from shafts that tapped the ancient buried beds of this same stream.

Nine hundred feet below the pond, the water gushes forth with tremendous force. Conducted downhill by a twenty-inch-diameter pipe, constricted to eleven inches at the exit point, the energy developed—nearly four hundred horsepower—was sufficient to light the mining town of Jardine and to power both its mills.

Jardine was a company town—enjoying periodic booms and suffering through the intervening busts. Each bust,

To construct the massive rock foundations to support the forty stamps of the Revenue Mill required six hundred perch of stone.

however, was but a pause, awaiting a new strike or a new set of investors.

Joe Brown caused the first excitement when he discovered placer gold in Bear Creek. That was in 1865, and the excitement increased when gold in quartz was found deep within Mineral Hill.

In 1884 a small stamp mill was built to replace the crude mule-drawn arrastra, but the rich veins ran out shortly, and operations ceased in 1886. Further prospecting brought new deposits to light. The mill was refurbished and enlarged, and operations resumed in 1890. Three years later the panic of '93 caused another shutdown.

Harry Bush arrived in 1898. He caused such vast changes that the town was named for him, but only momentarily.

*The cemetery at Jardine
says "Welcome."*

Three hotels, three mercantiles, three saloons, several houses
of ill repute, one church, and a school complemented the
great number of company buildings.

By 1899, the new mill was completed. Called the "Revenue," it held forty stamps. Each stamp weighed hundreds
of pounds, and each in turn was lifted five inches and permitted to fall on the coarse gold-bearing ore. Each stamp
dropped ninety times per minute. One of the few surviving
residents described the scene this way:

"With forty of them stamps going, the sound was more
than noise. You could feel it! Felt good, though—felt just
like a paycheck on Saturday night."

The severe pounding required massive rock foundations.
Six hundred perch of stone were used, a perch being almost
a cubic yard. The payroll ran nearly a quarter of a million
dollars per year. The town had a post office, and the population of the valley was measured in the thousands.

Mr. and Mrs. George W. Welcome were residents before
and after the big boom. When George died, a handsome
stone was placed at the head of his grave. Across the top,
in large letters, is printed one word—"WELCOME." It is
the first thing you see as you enter the cemetery. Some view-
ers are upset by the startling salutation, others are reas-
sured. Ripley's "Believe It or Not" referred to Jardine as
"the town where the cemetery says welcome."

The town was named "Jardine" about 1900, after a popular company superintendent. For three years the place enjoyed prosperity. By 1902 over a half million in gold had
been recovered. Other spurts of activity—there were twelve

Once erect and rolling free from mine to mill, this side-unloading
ore car rests leaning and inverted overlooking
the tracks it formerly traveled.

in all—resulted in a total take of 2.2 million gold between
1865 and 1926.

In 1926, arsenic ore was discovered in some of the tunnels. An addition was made to the lower mill to process the
new find. The final product obtained was arsenic trioxide,
a potent rat and bug killer, and a widely used paint pig-
ment. The mill processed nearly two hundred tons per day.

Some people claim that DDT killed the town. At least the
discovery of DDT ruined the market for arsenic as an in-

A rubber-coated "propeller" stirred reactants in tanks of the arsenic mill. The remains of the arsenic mill are in the left foreground, consisting of charred timbers and rusted machinery.

secticide. The plant closed in 1942, reopened briefly in 1944 to supply arsenic to the military, then closed again in 1945. A "mysterious" fire destroyed the arsenic plant in 1946, and the town's population went from few to almost none.

Twelve families now live in Jardine. Half of these are outfitters, guiding hunting and fishing parties into the unspoiled mountains to the north and east. Of the several hundred buildings, only a fraction remains. On the west side of the creek are a number of residences and an old store or

Looking north up the main street of Jardine's company town. The old store is on the left, the main offices at the end of the road on the right.

two. The town layout is accurately shown on the *Gardner, Montana, 15 minute topographic* map.

A dilapidated bridge permits adventurous access to a group of secluded shacks lying between the two forks of Bear Creek. An old sign at the bridge is accidentally appropriate:

"TRANSPASSING AT YOUR OWN RISK"

A windowless house displays a "WELCOME" sign over its hip-shot door. On the porch is a placard that proclaims: "RESERVED."

The east side was the company part of town. The two huge mills, an empty sawmill, and several dozen offices, cabins, and a store remain standing.

A few years ago, Richard and Jean Blankenship purchased the mining property. They found a number of build-

A nearly level track led from the tunnel mouth to the upper mill
The mill originally had forty stamps. Later it
was converted to a ball mill.

ings so far gone that they required destruction. Others are being repaired and put to use as guest houses. The Blankenships have hopes of installing a ski tow. Slopes and snow are already there in full abundance. The town is at an elevation of sixty-five hundred feet, and the hills on either side rise another two thousand feet.

The blacksmith shop, at the mine adit, or tunnel mouth, is in nearly perfect condition. It had an "improved" barrel stove. Fifty-gallon drums were commonly used as stoves, with a door in one end and a stovepipe at the rear. This stove, however, was a double-decker. The stovepipe led immediately into a second drum of equal size. The stovepipe was attached to the near end of this drum, and extended upward through the roof.

Near the smithy was an outhouse in an equally good state of preservation. The seating arrangement was uniquely simple. A four-inch-diameter log—smoothed by use—extended the full width of the structure. The twelve-foot width indicated a seating capacity of six men. The back

*Jardine, once a boom town, is quiet now. Quiet
as moonlight on still trees.*

rest was a three-inch-diameter log that also spanned the full
distance.

A changing room, near the tunnel mouth, was complete
with a twenty-four-foot shower. The lockers and benches
were all there. One locker contained a dusty, rotted towel.

Evidence all about indicated a massive human effort—
nature did not release her riches willingly. No fortunes
were made here, but there is still gold in Mineral Hill. Reserves are valued—by one investigator—at five million dollars. Most of the twenty tunnels in Mineral Hill have low-
grade ore visibly in contact.

Jardine is on the bust now, waiting for the next boom.
In the meantime the most industrious effort being carried
out on Bear Creek is the logging operation conducted by
the resident beavers. And somehow, one must agree—that
is the way it should be in Jardine.

Resembling a Spanish fort, the towers at Corwin were used by
spectators to observe vacationers in the hot mineral spring plunge.
The waters were said to have healing qualities.

CORWIN, MONTANA

The *Miner, Montana, 15 minute topographic* map revealed a number of prospective ghost towns: Miner, Carbella, Sphinx, Cinnabar, Aldridge, and Electric. All had been by-passed by the highway, several had deserted schools indicated, and one town, named Electric, was at the end of a dead-end road. Of these six possibilities, only two were worth visiting and photographing, but in the process of searching out these sites, I came across a third interesting remnant of early 1900 vintage.

Corwin (Springs) is located on the highway, but is nonetheless deserted. Perhaps it should not be called a town.

It was in reality a resort hotel, or spa, complete with hot mineral spring plunge, recreation parlor, and horse barns. Dr. F. E. Corwin built a seventy-two-room, three-story hotel on the site, and proclaimed the mineral baths a definite aid to healthy living. Special trains left Livingston, Montana, each weekend, carrying several hundred visitors and patients to the soothing comforts of Corwin Springs. The tracks paralleled Yellowstone River for many miles. Fishermen were given special treatment. A pull on the cord, and the train would stop, and three hundred vacationers would wish the angler good luck. The fishermen needed only to flag down the next train for a ride on in to Corwin, or for a return trip to Livingston.

The hotel burned to the ground on Thanksgiving Day, 1917. The plunge is still there, looking somewhat like a modern fort. Its parapets are empty, the doors are barred, and the pool is deserted.

The horse barns no longer cater to the dudes. There are no gentle equines here. Herds of domestic elk occupy the fields on either side. What a handsome steed an elk would make—and what a fantastic ride a dude would take!

ALDRIDGE, MONTANA

Sometimes nothing goes right. I turned left off Mol Heron Road, crossed the creek, and stopped at a trailer house to ask for permission and directions to Aldridge. Two rather large dogs took issue with my presence. I rolled up my map, pretended it was a weapon, and bluffed my way through. Yes, I could drive up through the gate if I wished. I would have to walk the last mile—would be better to go on up the main road a mile and a half, then walk cross-country.

The gate route sounded best to me, since it led past Aldridge Lake and the cemetery. At the gate I was confronted with a chain looped about the gate and the gatepost. It was secured by a railroad spike. After ten minutes of work, I concluded there was no way to get it open, and that the owner had made sure no one could gain access. As I drove out, the dogs barked with a derisive note.

Still confident, I pursued the second route, only to find that I had to ford Mol Heron Creek. It was high—too high to wade. In an hour the light was failing and I had found

Courtesy Rudy and Leo Planishek
An old picture of Happy Hollow, the uphill section of
Aldridge. Level building sites were rare.

no easy crossing. Then it began to rain. I retreated in four-wheel drive.

Luckily, I had learned of two old-timers who used to live in Aldridge. They had a vacation home in the area north of Corwin. It took only minutes to reach the highway and follow it north two miles to Cedar Creek.

Rudy and Leo Planishek, brothers, seventy-two and sixty-eight years respectively, offered me their kindest hospitality. We spent a long evening discussing the ghost towns of Aldridge and Electric. Their cabin is on the south bank of Cedar Creek, about three hundred yards east of U.S. Highway 89. They have the finest garden in Montana. Terraced, fertilized, and babied, the vegetables have no choice but to grow. Rudy even lets the stream water warm up in the barrel before he sprays it over the crop—something about not wanting to shock the tomatoes.

Rudy, the oldest, starts to tell each story. About the time he has warmed up, Leo takes over. Rudy shows a noticeable disappointment, but is soon captured by Leo's version of the story, and listens raptly to the end. Rudy jumps in with another, better story, only to have the ball stolen again. The two gentlemen surely understand one another. I asked how long they had lived together.

"Oh—just as long as we've been alive, about sixty-eight years—no, never married—both of us always did the same kind of work—coal mining mostly."

Aldridge was established in 1897, and Leo was born there in 1901. Rudy was four years old then,·and the two youngsters grew up in one of the toughest coal towns in Montana. The town was divided into two parts: "Happy Hollow," the residential area for the workers, most of whom were single, and, logically, "Downtown," which was five hundred feet down the hill below.

The company kept plenty of men employed by promising to help them bring a bride over from Austria. For $150 you could mail order a woman, but you took what you got, or forfeited your money. One hundred and fifty dollars was a hundred days' wages, and the company was happy to put you on a withholding plan.

Rudy and Leo have many stories to tell. One of them involved the kids of Aldridge and a portable whore house. A "traveling man," with two tents and two women, set up shop at the lower edge of town. Business started each evening at dark. "Like a drive-in movie," Leo added. The local women referred to the customers as "fence jumpers," and deplored the situation greatly. The kids got together and formed a plan to help solve the problem. A fifteen-gallon beer keg was stolen, filled with water, and aimed downhill at the two tents. It rolled straight and true, right up to the last rock in front of the tent. There it shattered and slanted harmlessly by. The vigilantes would have to try again!

The coal mined at Aldridge was sent downhill two miles to the town of Electric. There it was made into coke that was in turn used by the smelters to the north. An efficient tramway used the weight of the full buckets descending to pull the empty buckets back up the hill. No power other than gravity was required. A personnel-carrying cable car was also operated between the two towns, and was affectionately called the "Toonerville Trolley."

Rudy started work for the coal company in 1910, when he was thirteen years old. He worked for one month as a rock picker, and was looking forward to collecting his first pay. The mine closed just before payday, and Rudy still has not received his money!

The brothers were very disappointed that I had not reached the old townsite. I explained about the gate and the railroad spike, and then listened to the embarrassing truth. It is a standard latch in the area. Wiggle it just right and it pops open. It was too late and too muddy to return. Leo said there was only a shack or two left, and loaned me a couple of old pictures of the town.

Aldridge may be dead and nearly gone, but it is ever alive in the minds and words of the two fine gentlemen named "Planishek."

ELECTRIC, MONTANA

Founded by the Montana Coal and Coke Company in 1898, Electric was the downhill coking end of the two-town complex of Aldridge and Electric. Coal was originally shuttled downhill to Electric by a wooden flume. Wet coal had to be dried before it could be burned in closed kilns to form coke. The drying process took too long and the flume was inclined to freeze up on cold days. Consequently, in 1907, the tramway was built.

"Old" Charlie Dickson was hired as tram greaser. He rode the tram ten hours a day, greasing the tower wheels on the fly. Each noon he would hop off the bucket onto a convenient tower, climb down and eat his lunch. Shortly, the tramway would shut down for the noon hour. The tram stopped a bit early one day and stranded Charlie over Hoppe Creek, a thousand feet above the water. They say Charlie spent the balance of the day in close contact with a bottle of rye whiskey.

At Electric, the coal was loaded on small railroad cars and hauled by a dinky (a small locomotive) to the kilns. There were 254 kilns, each hemispherical in shape and about twelve feet in diameter. Railroad tracks ran above and alongside each row of kilns. Bricklayers, most of them Italians, would break open each oven. After cooling, "pullers" would hook out the coke, and load it on the cars. The ma-

With water spilling through an opening in the top and cascading over its curved side, this hemispherical kiln demonstrates suprising resistance to erosion. The oven is little changed since the last load of coke was pulled in 1910.

sons would then brick up the oven again. Another smaller hole would be broken in the top, six tons of coal poured in, and the oven bricked over to seal out the air. Heat from the former batch was enough to ignite the new charge. Seventy-

Charcoal kilns were constructed by Italian masons. Each held six tons of coal, which converted to coke in thirty-six to seventy-two hours.

two hours later the conversion was complete, and the process was repeated. Cheaper grades were given thirty-six hours. The coke was shipped by rail to the massive smelters at Anaconda, Montana.

Coke pullers were paid one dollar per oven. A good man could pull three a day. This did very little for a family's standard of living. Consequently, much of the town was a

The bachelor's cabin now stands in the middle of a horse corral, its roof well decorated with assorted sets of antlers.

near slum. Dotted with sheet-iron shacks, the working man's residential area was called "Tin Town."

The business district was impressive by contrast. A massive company store and saloon proclaimed in its false front in large block letters:

MONTANA COAL & COKE TRADING CO.
A STORE WITH EVERYTHING IN IT

The old log mule barn, built in 1897, sheltered the draft animals used to haul coal to, and coke from, the ovens at Electric.

Inside, canned goods reached from floor to ceiling. Minor competition came from the Fair & Square Grocery, but the lower prices were little inducement compared to the credit on wages offered by the company store.

There were nearly five hundred workers during the boom years, and the population of Electric was close to two thousand. The town was originally named "Horr," but in 1904, when an electric plant was installed, the name was changed to "Electric." Electric Peak, located a few miles south, and named for its unique ability to attract lightning, may have influenced the naming of the town.

In 1910 the mines at Aldridge ran into thin seams and low-grade coal. Company operations at both towns ceased. Aldridge died quickly, but Electric, on the traveled way, lasted considerably longer. Some buildings were moved out, others burned down and were never rebuilt, but the town remained a community gathering point until the school closed in 1945.

The townsite is now on the Charles and Annie Mikolich property, about two miles south of Corwin on the west side of the river. Of the several hundred original buildings, only the school, the Fair & Square Grocery, a bachelor's cabin, mule barn, and two strings of charcoal kilns survive. The store is now a garage. The bachelor's cabin is decorated with antlers, and located in the middle of a corral. It serves as a convenient rubbing post for livestock. The mule barn now shelters riding horses. Sagebrush, as high as your head, covers much of the traces of yesterday's endeavor. The red-brick kilns, stubbornly resisting the attack of time, make a fitting monument to the people who lived in the town of Electric.

MONTANA AREA 2

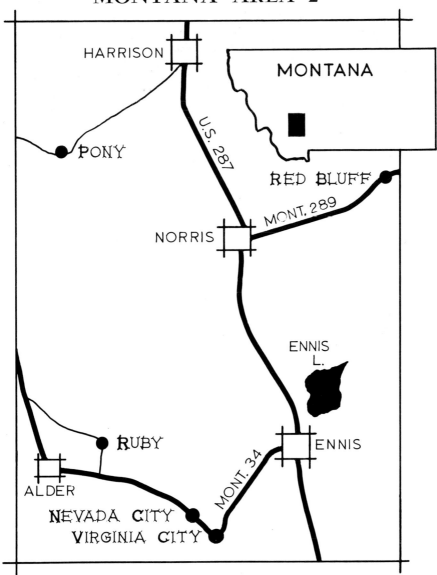

PONY, MONTANA

IT WAS A beautiful church, built solidly of hand-trimmed stone blocks. Its steeple lifted a sinner's eyes to heaven. It was an Episcopal Church, built as a memorial to a loved one

*The Episcopal church, built as a memorial, had a meager congregation.
Later, de-steepled, it became the I.O.O.F. Hall.*

of that faith. The church had no debts, and parishioners could rest assured no collection plate pressures would be applied. There was just one problem. Very few Episcopalians lived in Pony, and few of them attended. Eventually the church was sold to the Odd Fellows, who promptly removed the steeple and printed "IOOF" over the door.

The church stands in Pony today, its truncated tower reminding one of an elder, proud and dignified, watching his top hat blow down the hill.

Pony's history is full of strange stories and even stranger people. Gold was first located by a gent known mainly by his short stature, and his nickname, "Pony." He left town about the same time they named the town after him.

Pony sits astride the confluence of Pony Creek and Willow Creek, on the eastern slopes of the Tobacco Root Range. Harrison, Montana, and Highway 287 lie six miles to the northeast. The *Harrison, Montana, 15 minute topographic map* shows Pony and a number of nearby sites. The setting is beautiful, the road is good, and the people are friendly.

*Only the rock walls and a few heavy timbers remain at the Morris Mill
—a twenty stamper—and one of the last to cease operations.*

The original town—about two miles upstream—was called
"Strawberry." An outcrop of gold-bearing quartz was
found there, the vein widening to a generous ten feet at relatively shallow depths. The ore was rich enough to warrant
"on the spot" processing. By 1875, two mills were operating
two miles below the mine. A store was added and the people
of Strawberry drifted in. In 1877, streets were laid out.
Strawberry died as Pony sprang to life.

The mines slowly released their riches, and Pony grew.
It took twenty years to skim the cream, till only the low
grade was left in view. The Boss Tweed and the Clipper
mines had totaled more than two million in gold. Eventually
the mines shut down and people began to leave, but Pony
had one more good spurt left! An eastern syndicate bought
the Boss Tweed-Clipper property, and laid great plans for
development. One resident claims the mines were shot-
gunned—salted with gold and fired into the quartz. Whatever the reason, it was 1900 and prosperity had arrived
again. The new company built a massive three-story brick

*One of the many fine old residences in Pony. This one, with a
"Dutch door" over the porch, is still occupied.*

office building about one-half mile west of the town of Pony
on Willow Creek, and began the construction of a one-hun-
dred-stamp mill! The office is still there—good as new—but
no one seems to recall what happened to the mill.

It was a great moment in Pony's history. The townspeo-
ple built a $12,000 school. Main Street filled with stores.
Four fraternal orders vied for members. Three churches
tried vainly to counteract the evils of eleven saloons.

The bubble burst when ore tests revealed the truth. Not

In the foreground, the Isdell Mercantile. It had a horseshoe balcony for the display of goods. The building beyond housed a butcher shop.

only was the ore very low grade, but it was of a type that required more than simple crushing and separating. The developers were quick to leave. The original mineowners moved back to town and continued a modest milling operation. By 1918 the population had dwindled to three hundred. A few mines were still operating, their owners hopeful that the next blast would uncover a lost vein. The banker was still doing business—he would keep your money safe, but offered no interest. The last mine closed in 1922.

*From the left: the Schriner Building, with a large Rex Flour billboard
painted on the front; the Hoffer Hardware; and next a rooming
house-saloon combination with rooms on the second floor.
In the background, a multi-use fraternal building.*

Nearly a half a century has passed. Now only a few families live in Pony. It is a popular site to visit. The tourists often outnumber the residents. The Morris State Bank, standing alone at the southwest corner of the main intersection, is of particular interest. Two stories high, with full basement, the brick structure shows little sign of deterioration. Gilt lettering on the windows reads:

INFORMATION   U.S. COMMISSIONER
PROSPECTS   NOTARY PUBLIC
MINES   JAMES A. FLINT

Spindle-back chairs and desks are still in place and visible through the windows. Downstairs is a tonsorial parlor, its bathtub dry and dusty.

Half a block east, and across the street, are two more deserted buildings. The wooden structure was once a butcher shop. The cooler is open and empty of ice. A "teller cage" type room was apparently occupied by the bookkeeper. Be-

This strange coded message was chiseled into stone by a former marshal of Pony. The meaningless symbols were apparently designed to excite the gullible treasure seeker.

side the butcher shop is the Isdell Mercantile, a brick building with high arched windows. Inside, a horseshoe balcony provides two stories of shelving. Scattered all about are receipts from the years 1910 to 1933. One shipping statement, dated November 11, 1910, was for "Superior Oak Harness" that was shipped in from Marshal Wells, Duluth, Minnesota.

Farther east, and across the street, are four more deserted buildings. First is the Schriner Building, with a large "Rex Flour" billboard painted on its front. Only the front wall remains standing. Next is the old Hoffer Hardware, and then the Rooming House–Saloon combination. Nearby is a two story brick multi-purpose fraternal club building.

Marshal William B. Landon was well known in the Pony area—not for his law enforcement, but for his strange passion for chiseling rock. He apparently became disenchanted with the neighboring town of Potosi. Selecting a large boulder beside the road about a mile out of Potosi, he chiseled on it in bold letters:

"ONE MILE TO HELL"

West of Pony, on the north side of the Strawberry Mill Road, is another of his masterpieces. The rock is opposite the stream, where the stream is closest to the road, and is between the town dump and the cattle guard. The rock is a flat piece of granite, about four by seven feet. On it he has inscribed some strange letters, unlike any in our alphabet—also a maltese cross, his initials, and the date 1921. He confided to friends that it was just a hoax, to make others think it was a secret treasure map. Like the old lady who liked blueberry muffins—and saved up an entire attic full —the old marshal just liked to carve rock. He even carved his own tombstone, and the town folk buried him beside it.

Two ghosts are said to walk the town at night. If true, then the ghost of William B. Landon must assuredly be one of them!

RED BLUFF, MONTANA

The *Norris, Montana, 15 minute topographic* map shows Red Bluff as a town with cemetery, empty buildings, and nearby abandoned mines. The deserted mines were prime indication that Red Bluff would be a ghost town. Inspection showed that Red Bluff had long since passed through the

Once a boardinghouse for miners, this solidly built rock structure has served as a residence, hotel, and now a research station.

"ghost" stage, and was now in its third "reincarnation."

Prior to 1864, Red Bluff was a stage stop on the old Bozeman Cutoff. Located on Hot Springs Creek, at the upper end of a narrow five-mile canyon, it was a popular place to gulp a bracer before facing the rigors of the road.

In 1864 a large two-story stone building was built on the north side of the thoroughfare. The number of chimneys indicates that each room had a fireplace or stove. The structure served as a boardinghouse for miners from 1870 to 1900 or so, then was converted to a residence. Later, it became a hotel. Now it holds the offices of Red Bluff Research Station of Montana State University.

The town "died" in 1920, but in its prime it had a bank, many residences, and (reportedly) one thousand citizens. Now only the stone hotel, a mine tunnel, a few old shacks and the cemetery are left.

The cemetery is still in use, and well kept. The older section has some interesting headstones:

Nothing is plumb at the Boaz Mine. Even the weeds grow on the bias

The gallows frame over the Boaz Mine has a built-in ladder. A makeshift fence protects cattle from falling into the five-hundred-foot-deep shaft.

This four-place seesaw gave long service. Located just behind the Boaz shaft, it may have been, originally, a transformer support.

A unique heat ventilator, adjacent to the chimney, served to keep the cook cool and happy at the Peanuts Mine cookhouse.

Joseph Walbank
of Keighly, England
Died Age 60
Nov 10 1888

Jemima T. Foster
1845-1904
Faithful to the End

—and this tearful poem on the grave of a little girl who
died at age nine:

Ere Sin Could Harm or Sorrow Fade
Death Came With Friendly Care
The Opening Bud To Heaven Conveyed
And Bade It Blossom There.

Red Bluff had ten great years. From 1870 to 1880 the
Boaz Mine brought $200,000 worth of silver and gold to
the surface. The Josephine did as well. The Gold Cup, Wa-
terlode, Helene, and Grubstake were all operating multiple
shifts.

Located two miles south of Red Bluff, the long dormant
Boaz Mine was revived briefly in 1941 and 1948. Both times
it failed to pay out. Here a fifty-ton cyanide mill once
spewed forth is viscous yellow waste. A dam across a small
stream provided still water, permitting the solids to settle
out. The dam is gone, but the solid yellow shelf of sediment
remains. At the mine proper, a beautifully square shaft,
about eight feet on a side, extends five hundred feet downward. Side drifts exit at the one hundred sixty-five, two
hundred sixty-five, three hundred sixty-five and five hundred
foot levels. Poorly mounted on their foundations, the buildings have taken on considerable list. Each has its own
personality, the overall effect being that of an amusement
park fun house. At the uphill end of the mine complex, a
large machine shop stands, its walls gone, but the roof pro-
viding welcome shade for a dozen white-faced cattle.

The mine was run by an engineer with commendable
imagination. When electricity came in, the steam boiler was
converted to a hot-water heater. A four-place teeter-totter,
pivoted on a power pole, kept the kids happy. Perhaps it
was originally a transformer support, but the curved
grooves worn in the center pole could only have been caused
by hours of play.

Just down the hill adjoining the Boaz, are the shafts of
the Peanuts Mine. Several buildings are there, one of them

obviously a cookhouse. The stove is gone, but the chimney stands; and just in front of the chimney, squarely above the stove location, is another innovation quite ahead of its time. A four-by-four cupola, about six feet high, contains screened-in louvres designed to permit the escape of heat. The food must have been good. Only a good cook deserved such deluxe facilities.

A typical residence in Virginia City, complete with a two-sided porch designed to entrap the breezes, however vagrant.

VIRGINIA CITY, MONTANA

The judge agreed the place called Alder Creek should have an official name. But "Varina?" After the wife of Jeff Davis? It was 1864, and no Northern judge would certify such a name. He wrote out "Virginia" instead, and "Virginia City" it became.

In one year it was a full-blown town, with hotels, schools, fire department, newspaper, opera house, and hundreds of homes. Buildings were going up at the incredible rate of one hundred each week, and the population reached the ten thousand mark. It became the capital city in 1865. Three-fourths of a mile long, four streets wide—and nearly every lot sold!

The original Overland Stage Office now performs much the same function it did in 1865. Coffee, snacks, and full-course meals are available to the traveler.

One of the many deserted mine shacks that overlook Virginia City. The road to this site is suited only to four-wheel-drive vehicles.

Money was abundant, and a multitude of crooks moved in to take their share. One hundred and ninety murders occurred in seven months. Vigilantes caught up with and hung five suspects, using the conveniently exposed beams of a half-finished store. Another was hung in Nevada City, and a few more, including the ringleader, were dispatched in Bannack. As in an early silent Western, the sheriff of Bannack was found to be the mastermind. His name was "Plummer," so the gang, whose members had now fled— or were dead, was finally given a name—the "Plummer Gang."

The Chinese laundry operators catered especially to the miners. Pant pockets were thoroughly scrubbed, and the wash water then panned. The gold recovered often exceeded the fee charged for washing. Oriental laborers moved in on the placers as quickly as the miners deserted them. Soon there were six hundred Chinese panning gold,

*One hundred years ago gunsmith shops were as common as
jewelry stores are today. The giant gun left no
doubt as to the store's function.*

Some shops—like this Wells Fargo Express Office—are complete with lifelike manikins. The "lady" at the left may be inquiring as to passage to a nearby town. Note the strongboxes, one leather bound, the other reinforced with iron bands.

happy to glean the trace of riches left by the first wave of gold seekers. By 1895, even the Chinese gave up, and the town shrank to six hundred. Few people lived the year round in Virginia City after 1920.

In 1946, the town caught the attention of State Senator and millionaire rancher Charles Bovey. He made a hobby of restoring the town to its original glory. Some saloons, stores, cafes, and one hotel went back in business, making as few changes as possible, with a code of accurate reconstruction carefully imposed. Some stores were restocked with their original merchandise.

The stage office, barbershop, library, and livery were repaired and refurbished. By 1968, the entire town was one big functioning museum.

*Typical of the restored buildings on Main Street, this store is a
complete museum, filled with much of its original stock.*

*The Gilbert Brewery in Daylight Gulch—the northeastern part of
Virginia City—boasted its own private beer garden.*

There was gold in Virginia City again. It walked on two
legs and was called "tourist." Happily, the prices were not
high and the sights were priceless. It was truly an experience to walk down Wallace Street, especially in the
quiet of early morning.

Things changed in 1968. Virginia City lost much of its
charm when a modern store was built at the edge of town.
In front of the store, a gigantic plywood cowboy now shouts
commercialism down the length of Wallace Street. The
echoes fall painfully upon the ears of those who have tried
so hard to preserve the spirit of 1864.

*Although no railroad served Nevada City during gold-mining days,
this little engine is one of the precious "relics of
the era" that decorate the town.*

NEVADA CITY, MONTANA

Five hundred vigilantes gathered around John "The Hat"
Dolan, and draped a noose about his neck. Four thousand
citizens watched as the victim was raised, his feet resting
precariously on a board held unfirmly by his captors. Dolan
admitted the crime, but asked for mercy, as he was drunk
at the time. The board tilted, and "The Hat" died quickly.
The crowd, sympathetic toward the victim, surged forward,
but the sound of five hundred revolvers being cocked changed
their collective mind. They retreated in haste.

That was Nevada City, Montana, in 1864. The same year,

*Much of Nevada City is reconstructed and many of the items on display
are borrowed from other locales. This old stagecoach is
one of the exceptions. It made many trips on
the Virginia City—Salt Lake run.*

eighteen hundred citizens voted in the town's first election.
Born of the same boom that spawned Virginia City, and located a short two miles to the west, Nevada City was destined to a lively but abbreviated existence. Seventy million
in gold was panned in the vicinity. The extraction took only
four years, and when the gold was gone, most of the population drifted to richer deposits. Much of the town was left
vacant. The remaining citizens used many of the unoccupied buildings for firewood. The Adelphi Hall, Masonic
Temple, the Hotel, and even the Star Bakery and Saloon
went up in smoke. The latter had advertised: "An honest

Few genuine two-story outhouses are intact today. This reconstructed
outhouse is not a working model but serves to illustrate
the grand pre-plumbing achievement of 1900.

loaf . . . and something to wash it down." Charles Bovey,
who headed the restoration of Virginia City, also instigated
the reconstruction of Nevada City. The aim here was quite
different. Few of the buildings are original structures.
Some have been moved in, others have been built from
scratch to resemble the original. The contents of these buildings are not intended to be authentic. One holds a collection
of old mechanical bands. A quarter in the slot will give you

all the noise you want. Although no train ever passed through the town, the collection of memorabilia assembled here includes a number of old steam engines, coaches, and mixed rolling stock.

One of the few remaining two-story outhouses is attached to the rear of the hotel. The outhouse is not a working model. It is a rather crude reconstruction of the real thing. This type of annex was usually built with an offset so that deposits made at the upper level would pass behind the occupant at the ground level. The first visit to the lower floor during multiple use was claimed to be a harrowing experience.

RUBY, MONTANA

The gold bars had been poured especially shallow. They fitted tightly into the pockets attached to the stout leather harness. Built like a double-breasted Sam Browne belt, the shoulder straps accepted and distributed the weight of the heavy metal. The suit vest was put on next, and tightly buttoned. A hideaway gun was strapped on. After donning coat and hat, the messenger stepped into the sun, mounted his horse and rode out of the town of Ruby. The carrier was one of the owners of the Conrey Placer Mining Company. Millions of dollars in gold were delivered to the nearest bank by "gold vest courier" without a single robbery attempted!

Nearly ten million dollars in gold were dredged here. A drastic turnabout for a small community that began as a poor farm.

The Conrey Placer Mining Company was formed soon after geologist N. S. Shaler determined the extent of gold in the gravel beds of Alder Creek. He and Gordon McKay of Boston purchased the Conrey Ranch and proceeded to lay plans for deep dredging. The miners of 1864 had worked the area over, and later the Chinese reworked it. Observers had little hopes for the third effort, but it paid off handsomely. Harvard University shared in the profits when the McKay estate was settled.

The brick building that was the poor-farm hospital became the company office. Most of the paupers' shacks—one-room chinked log structures with sod roofs—became quarters for employees. The powerhouse, where twelve water-cooled transformers once hummed twenty-four hours a day,

The Ruby Stables, an "in town livery," was particularly convenient for keeping the company horses used to transport gold to the nearest bank.

Only one of the pre-1890 paupers' houses is still intact. The lock-joint corners show little sign of weakening, and the door jamb is remarkably plumb.

In the foreground, the old brick company office, once the poor-farm hospital. Beyond is the retort building where gold was melted and poured into ingots.

Geese with young provide stubborn opposition to trespassers. The corrugated metal-coated building once held a dozen water-cooled electrical transformers.

Steam dredges, no longer in existence, consumed wood at a rate of twenty cords per day. Electric motors replaced the steam engines in 1906.

was later converted to a barn. A three-story, ten-room hotel-boardinghouse was built, three saloons sprang up, and a butcher moved to town and opened shop. There were two general stores, a post office, dance hall, and a three-room schoolhouse. The population held steady at five hundred from 1900 to 1922. Since that time, a number of fires have destroyed some buildings, but the mining office, hotel, stable, a pauper's cabin, powerhouse, retort building, and several residences are standing quite undisturbed. The retort building, with its furnace and vault, is preserved intact. Ingot molds, lifting tongs, ovens, mercury bottles, overhead tracks, and even a burglar alarm button can still be found inside. The walk-in vault, built of concrete walls thirty inches thick, holds a mixed bag of valuables. Just above the potatoes (it doesn't freeze inside the vault), is a delicate weighing balance and a set of brass scale weights. One weight is marked "12 OUZ-TROY," and is a one-pound weight measured in the Troy system. The hideaway gun is still there. Also the leather harness used to secure the hidden gold bars. For bigger and bolder shipments, a pair of saddle bags were employed, capable of holding a full-sized ingot on each side. The original equipment and the old company buildings are owned and carefully preserved by Lowell Gilman. Lowell's father was company superintendent when the effort was abandoned.

Like the ribs of a decayed monster, the timbers of an old dredge mark the spot where activities ceased.

Somewhere between eight and ten million dollars' worth of gold and platinum was melted and poured into ingots. That represents nearly seventy tons of precious metal. Standard ingots weighed sixty to eighty pounds and were a bit larger than a brick. Hideaway bars weighed about one-fourth as much, and were about the size of a bar of soap.

The first dredge, or gold boat, was named "Maggie A. Gibson." It operated for five years, gulping twenty cords of wood each day. The gravel reserves seemed endless, and a succession of dredges was built, each one larger and more voracious in appetite than its predecessor.

Electric power was available in 1906, and new plans were drawn for a mammoth "all electrical" machine. It was to be larger than any other dredge in existence.

Building a dredge was a complex operation. First, horses and drag lines were employed to dig a dry pond. Timbers were laid out at the deepest point, and the planking bolted on. As soon as the joints were packed with oakum, water was admitted to the pond. Complete with superstructure and machinery, the monster had a weight of 4,070,000 pounds. It required thirty-three carloads of lumber and forty-two carloads of machinery. It could pump twelve

A shiny cup on an old pump rod casts a reflection enhanced by the camera's lens.

thousand gallons of water and dig three hundred and thirty cubic feet of gravel per minute. The buckets were linked into an endless chain, connected with link pins eight inches in diameter. The dredge could dig fifty feet deep. It wandered along in a zigzag manner, digging a swath three hundred feet wide, moving ten thousand cubic yards per day. It could make a profit on just three cents' worth of gold per cubic yard! Eight men ran the dredge, while two others drilled test holes to determine the most profitable direction for the dredge to take. The dredges ate up, digested, and redeposited more than a square mile of land. The location and extent of operations are clearly shown on the *Alder, Montana, 7½ minute topographic* map.

The dredged stream no longer knows its own bed. Each spring it finds a new path. Each dredge had carried its own pond with it as it slowly toured the basin, and the ponds that remain mark the scenes of their final efforts.

Amid the cattails can be found the bonelike remains of the long dead behemoths that laid this land in ugly waste. Nature's retaliation is slow, but ever sure. Windblown soil, trapped in the rocky windrows permits a few plants to gain a foothold. Quickly, measured by nature's clock, the banks of Alder Creek will again become green, and flowers will once more spark the meadows with color.

MONTANA AREA 3

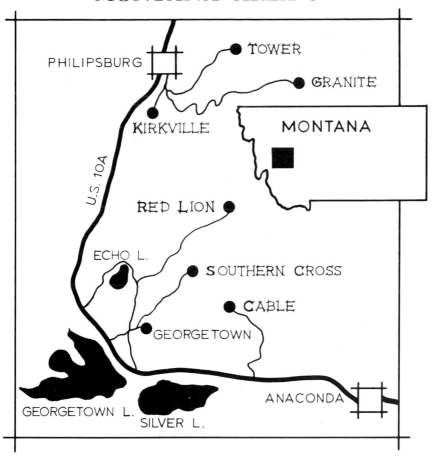

PHILIPSBURG

TOWER

GRANITE

MONTANA

KIRKVILLE

U.S. 10A

RED LION

ECHO L.

SOUTHERN CROSS

CABLE

GEORGETOWN

GEORGETOWN L.

SILVER L.

ANACONDA

CABLE, MONTANA

Maps are generally a big help, but at Cable, the carto-
graphic aid was a complete bust. I was using the 1908 edition (revised, 1949) of the *Philipsburg, Montana, 30 minute topographic map*. It failed to show the new roads (that
is to be expected), but it showed some roads that did not
exist, and located others erroneously. Cable wasn't hard to
find, but attempts to pass through to Southern Cross (another ghost town) resulted in my becoming hopelessly confused. I was about to pass by the mill at Cable for the fourth
time when I decided to give up, concentrate on Cable, and
perhaps find Southern Cross the next day via some other

*Built in 1899, this deluxe barn, with full basement, catered to the
welfare of the local bird population in an effort
to control the insect problem.*

more understandable route. I grabbed my cameras, slammed
the door and started walking up the deserted gravel road,
kicking at loose rocks along the way. My frustrations lessened as I banged away with increasing vigor. The tra-
jectories were improving and I was beginning to take rather
loud vocal pride in my work. That's when I looked up. A
man was standing by the mine entrance—staring at me. I
approached, considerably embarrassed.

The Cable Mill is conveniently located just a few hundred feet from the mine entrance. It was a choice place to work, where high-grading was widespread and lucrative.

"You lost? Saw you go by three times."

"No," I answered, "but I sure can't find Southern Cross."

He was a kind man, hardly grinned at all. He gave me all the right instructions, but I was so red-faced and confused that nothing made sense.

Although Cable is not one of my favorite sites, it does have an undeniable ghostliness. On the west side of Cable Creek there are three very old cabins, complete with split log steps —nicely smoothed and firmly placed. The cabins show a recent (1930 or so) renovation with interior paneling and modern fixtures. More recently, the inevitable vandalism has taken its toll.

Next to the cabins, on the downhill side, is a huge barn. A cupola-birdhouse-lightning rod combination rides the

Core samples taken in a last-ditch effort to regain a lost vein are racked from floor to ceiling in the assay office adjacent to the mill.

ridge. More accommodations for birds—probably martins —are spread across the front of the barn. With perching shelves on the outside and boxed-in houses extending through to the inside, nothing, it seemed, was too good for the feathered friends. Outside of citronella and flyswatters, birds were the most effective means of mosquito control.

Inside the barn, a flight of steps with a smoothly worn handrail leads to the hayloft and grain bins. On the main floor are stalls for draft animals. The basement level has more stalls and provisions for other animals such as cows, pigs, goats, and chickens.

The huge mill is across the creek and up the hill a few hundred yards. In a shaky state of repair, it groans in the wind, shedding a few of its remaining shingles with each gust. Thousands of tons of ore passed through this mill. Large mine dumps indicate extensive working underground.

Gold at Cable was discovered quite by accident. A deep shaft was being dug to intercept a suspected vein at considable depth. One corner of the shaft nicked a gold-rich quartz vein at very shallow depth.

Subsequent filing of claims failed to bring the expected stampede, due perhaps to a number of previous false alarms. A year later, in 1868, the forty-ton mill was built and the Atlantic Cable Lode began to pay off. A severe cave-in caused a temporary shutdown in 1869. A second strike in 1873 revived the failing community, but it, too, found the end of the vein. In 1878, the town dwindled to a population of one. A third strike brought in a boom that lasted from 1883 to 1891 and netted three million in gold, after high-grading. A number of former employees—it has been reported—suddenly bought fine homes and fancy horses. Reopened in 1902, the mining efforts were expanded to three shifts in 1906, then faded slowly. All work ceased in 1940.

Now, in 1969, the new owner has sent a mining engineer out to inspect the remaining ore deposits. The engineer has found that all manner of strange people visit the site, including odd characters, carrying cameras, who kick gravel and talk to themselves.

RED LION, MONTANA

Sometimes it is fun to enter a ghost town with no prior knowledge. Then, after a careful inspection, compare one's findings with the reports of others. At Red Lion there is no choice, since very little has been written on this community.

A few bare facts are available. One of the two mills at the site was built in 1890 and was horribly inefficient. The Hanna tunnel was deep, and its ores were rich in gold, iron, and copper. A tramway, nearly a mile long, was built in 1906, at which time two hundred men worked at the mine-mill complex.

The camp is about seven miles northeast of Georgetown, accessible by a well-signed gravel road and well indicated

A nineteenth-century forerunner to the modern tri-level home.
From the entry you step down to the sunken living room.

on the same *Philipsburg map* used to locate Cable. To the
right of the road, where it crosses Flint Creek, there are a
number of broken-down log shacks and a few rock foundations. This is Red Lion. At first it looks like seven wasted
miles, but close inspection reveals some intriguing details.

A tunnel is visible to the right (or south) of the cabins,
and water pours from it. The flow is considerable, causing
Flint Creek—when joined—to double in size. This is probably the seven-hundred-foot-deep Hanna tunnel. A king-
size pump must have been used to keep it de-watered.

The cabins at the center of camp are largely collapsed.
The ground is soggy all about, not conducive to permanent
construction. One building shows the remains of hearth and
anvil bases, and was probably a blacksmith shop. Another
seems to have been a dance hall or saloon, and a third building, equipped with shelves, was likely a mercantile.

The mill and tramway are now merely leveled mounds
of wood and bent metal. Just up Flint Creek from the millsite is an old log cabin. Old as far as age is concerned, but

*This boardinghouse had an outside stairway and a covered walk. Just
a few feet away, the clear waters of Flint Creek tumbled by.*

brand-new in design. Dozens of modern tri-level homes use
the same floor plan. Sagging four ways from square, its
corner lock joints feel the strain and slowly readjust. Buildings this stout seldom collapse. They just ease their way
down like a tired old man making ready for bed.

Near the tri-level cabin is a marvelous old two-story
boardinghouse, its outside stairway connecting with an
elevated boardwalk. Braced with timbers, the broad eaves
still protect the walkways from rain and snow. The second
floor was divided into bunk rooms and since there were no
chimneys, one might assume they were unheated. At 7,300
feet altitude, the winters can get mighty frosty. The kitch-
en downstairs was probably the winter social center.

A thorough search of the buildings revealed no receipts,
newspapers, or other records that might give further clues
to the history of Red Lion. Somewhere there is an old-timer
who knows all about the place and can string a hundred
stories together in a way that would bring momentary life
to this old camp.

*The old Chicago Mine, only recently abandoned, is still complete
with landing stage, head frame, and hoist house.*

TOWER, MONTANA

Roads emanate from Philipsburg like the arms of a nervous octopus. The *Philipsburg, Montana, 30 minute topographic* map is great for selecting sites to visit, but of little value in determining which road to take. If you can find the gravel road past the hospital and substation in southeast Philipsburg, follow it south, then east, remaining on the main road for two miles, you might reach Tower. The steep winding road overlooks Philipsburg for the first mile, then

*This angle bay window caught the warmth of the sun at all times of
the day. It was the envy of every housewife in Tower.*

heads up the valley. Shortly you pass between a deserted mine and mill, probably the Speckled Trout, then head for a yellow mine dump. At this point the road splits. The right-hand route curls around and climbs to the True Fissure Mine. The left route takes you up the main street of Tower. Main Street is the only street in town. In moments you have passed several dozen cabins that make up the town of Tower, and are at the Chicago Mine. Recently active, it remains complete with stage, cable, hoist, and bucket.

On the left, heading back into town, is a fine old house that sports a three-sided angle bay window. Now weathered to a paintless gray, boards warped and decayed, it still retains the suggestion of past beauty.

Farther down the street is an old store, false-fronted and log-sided. Once used as a garage, it now lies open and deserted.

It is very quiet here. Not a soul is in town, yet there are signs of occupancy. A sign on one door warns someone not to swipe anything since he was seen the first time. Another cabin has a number of dynamite fuses, already capped, hanging by the screen door. Behind one house is an old mine tunnel, fitted with a heavy wooden door. Cold air billows forth when it is opened, indicating that it might be used for cold storage.

Tower never was a big town. Built originally to accommodate mill workers, it struggled along, imitating the boom and bust of nearby Philipsburg. The first well-known mine was the "Speckled Trout," discovered in about 1870. A mill was built in 1875, and a boardinghouse constructed to accommodate its workers. Later, the Algonquin Mine, rich in silver, was developed just south of the "Trout." Charlemagne Tower, for whom the town was named, was one of the prime investors in the early mines. During World War I manganese was found here. The military demand was quickly filled, and the mining of manganese dropped off until other uses of the metal could be found. By 1940, it was in demand once more, particularly as an ingredient necessary to the manufacture of improved dry cells. The True Fissure Mine went back into production and is still in operation.

While I had walked through Tower observing its quiet scenery, deep below my feet there was activity. Men of the True Fissure were mucking a gooey gray mass of ore, shoveling it into ore cars, and trundling the cars to the shaft for hoisting.

The dry air, common in Montana, has warped the siding on this false-fronted store. Converted to a garge, the building leans heavily toward the horizontal.

I learned of the operation from the hoisting engineer. The shaft house is located high on the hill above town. Inside, the engineer sits with control levers and gigantic drums of cable in front of him. Through the window he could see the top of the shaft. On a two-foot-diameter dial, he could read the stage location. At the moment, he was slowing the stage for a stop at the one-thousand-foot level. He could bring it close, but for exact matching of levels he relied on signals from below. The bells dinged, and he lowered the stage a few inches. Later, after another series of signals, he started the stage up, with two tons of ore on board. At eight hundred feet per minute, the load was quickly topside, and being pushed to a point just over the bed of a dump truck. The unloader tripped each car in turn so that it spilled into the vehicle.

Later I visited the smithy. He told me of his work, stressing the fact that the mine had a water problem requiring one thousand gallons a minute to be pumped out, day and night. That, along with occasional mechanical breakdowns, kept him busy.

Tower is a different sort of ghost town—deserted, but with activity far below and high above on the hill. There is no noise except the periodic clang of ore cars being dumped. The modern mining of manganese is but a faint echo of yesterday's exciting pursuit of silver and gold.

The last resident of Granite lived in this house. The picket fence encloses a random collection of memorabilia.

GRANITE, MONTANA

The Queen City! The Silver Capital of the World! Each month a quarter million dollars' worth of silver was torn from the earth. The rich ores poured out of the Granite and Bi-Metallic shafts at an increasing rate. Thirty million in silver in ten years—then came the crash!

August 1, 1893, was a sad day in Granite. Orders came that day to shut down the mine. Within hours the road to Philipsburg was filled as thousands fled down the hill. Jobs

The large company hospital was designed to hold victims of
major disasters. Some miners complained of too
much cure and too little prevention.

might still be open in Philipsburg, and each man wanted to
be first in line. Six hundred hardy souls remained behind to
enjoy the hollow luxuries of Granite, the fastest dying ghost
town in the west.

There had been luxuries in Granite, for Granite had been
a fancy town. The three-story Miners Union Hall would be
quiet now, its springy maple dance floor no longer pulsing
to the rhythm of happy feet. The staff of doctors would have
few patients in the overlarge company hospital. A few shift
bosses might use the heated plunge, but the laughter of hard-
working men would not be there. The four church congre-
gations were confronted by bewildered parsons. The hotel
and roller rink closed the first week. Eighteen saloons did

The Miners Union Hall stands as a memorial to the greatness of Granite. The gravel was once a prime residential street.

little business. They closed not one by one—more like four by four. Nourished by a few retired miners and the skeleton crew at the mine, the town of Granite hibernated in hopes that rising silver prices might sometime warm it once again to life.

The map used for Cable, Tower, and Red Lion, also covers the Granite area. Again the roads are confusing. Leave Philipsburg as if heading for Tower, but make an abrupt right turn before passing the last five or six houses. The road crosses the railroad twice, then forks to the right and proceeds uphill. Although serpentine, the four-mile road to Granite is easily managed by ordinary passenger vehicle.

On the right, as you enter Granite, there is an old house

*Part of the old mill is seen through the wreckage of a "house of ill
fame." The street was appropriately named "Silk Stocking Row."*

The Granite Mill, closed in 1889, held twenty stamps. A shortage of water limited its capacity, causing it to be replaced with a larger mill located two miles south on Fred Burr Creek.

surrounded by a rickety picket fence. Not long ago its resident installed a television set. The antenna still perches atop the roof—totally incongruous with the structure beneath. In this house lived the "grand old lady of Granite," the last resident. She died in 1968.

A narrow gravel road to the left leads to the main part of town. On the right is the two-story hospital, its covered porch half gone, the chimney falling down, and the shingles all but gone. Shortly, a left turn leads to the old Miners Union Hall—a magnificent remnant! It stands alone and lonely, intact in front, in complete shambles at the rear. Vandals have broken the windows and stolen the fixtures. To the east are a number of old residences. A few have walk-in coolers dug into the hill behind. Some miners started with a rock-walled, sod-roofed dugout, and graduated later into "sawed board" homes, and used the sod house for storage. Most of the wooden structures are now gone, but many rock soddies remain.

Farther up the hill and to the right are, in order, an old brick bank vault, the rock company house, and several broken-down "houses of ill fame." The street was named "Silk Stocking Row." The close proximity of the two enterprises would indicate that the company condoned and controlled this facet of evening entertainment. Granite was most thoroughly a "Company Town."

Located just above, and overlooking the town, are the extensive stone foundations of the old Granite Mill. Like hornets' nests, coke ovens nestle in the rock foundations. Burned timbers lean aslant, their fire-blackened metal fittings standing out prominently.

A shiny corrugated metal building stands in the tiny basin where once the famous "Granite and Bi-Metallic" shafts poured forth their wealth. Inside, the hoist engineer waits for the signal to raise the stage. There are men below checking every stope and drift. The shaft has been cleared to eighteen hundred feet, and there are plans to go down another seven hundred feet. The new owners, Bi-Metallic of Heccla, are well acquainted with the mine's past production, and are gambling that "there's more where that came from."

KIRKVILLE (CLARK), MONTANA

Few people visit Kirkville, I would have passed it by, had it not been for the cherished (and dog-eared by now) *Philipsburg, Montana, 30 minute topographic map*. It clearly shows a double railroad spur, a number of buildings, and a flume—all indications of a community that was once a going concern.

Situated one mile south of Philipsburg, the town of Kirkville is easily located—just follow the railroad tracks to the large twin chimneys. The road dead-ends at the vacant two-story brick office building of the Bi-Metallic Mining Company.

The adjacent mill was built in 1888 to handle the ores from Granite. A two-mile tramway brought ore down in quarter-ton lots and returned wood and coal to Granite. Originally a fifty-stamp mill, it was quickly enlarged to one hundred stamps capable of handling two hundred tons of ore per day.

The mill was gigantic—eight levels, one hundred and fifty feet wide and nearly four hundred feet long. It re-

*Tumbled shacks and wagon wheels embedded in the silt of old tailing
ponds echo the inert state of the carpentry and
blacksmith shops behind.*

quired five hundred employees to operate. The ores were
crushed in beds of mercury—the stamps splashing the expensive amalgamating agent freely onto the floor. Five hundred employees made quite a town. Bachelors lived in the
many rooming houses. Families built residences just east
of the mill. A number of workers lived in Philipsburg, but
in spite of this, Kirkville was the third largest town in the
area.

Sometime after 1908, the town was renamed "Clark," but
by then activities had nearly ceased. In 1967 the mill
burned to the ground. During the intervening years, most
of the residences have burned or been moved, yet there is
much left to see in Kirkville!

Straw-boss barracks located behind the company office building had a deluxe covered porch. The building held apartments, each with facilities for four men.

Beside the tracks are several large machine shops and warehouses full of ore cars, track, ore buckets, stages, and all manner of spare parts. Strung on down the line are the assay office and pouring room. Both are complete, minus only the smaller movable equipment. The pouring room has large kilns, ladles, scales, and a steel-doored walk-in vault with numerous hefty shelves. Heavy bars of silver once rested here, row upon valuable row.

A few yards farther, at the burned-over mill, "second effort" mining is going on. It is a two-man operation. One man digs out the earth from under the old amalgamator stamps and dumps it into a hopper. The second man feeds the earth into a rotary washer where the coarse material

A water-carrying flume passing behind the shops was built like a covered half round barrel, with semicircular bolts acting as hoops.

drops out. The fine sediments zigzag their way down a long wooden sluice, or long tom, leaving shiny droplets of mercury in each crevice. When mercury shows up at the bottom of the sluice, it is time to shut down and clean up. The sloppy techniques of 1890 are paying off today.

Across the tracks are the old carpenter and blacksmith shops. A long wooden flume runs behind the buildings. In front are extensive tailing ponds. Half buried in the sediments are an outhouse, collapsed shed, and several wagon wheels.

As in an old travelogue, the setting sun cast a glow upon the face of the burned-over mill. Shortly the darkening skies were dimly relit as the moon rose, heavily shrouded with clouds. The grandeur of 1890 seemed to return. The mill looked whole again.

The moon, the towering chimneys, the threatening skies, all combined to create a mood not easily shrugged. Suddenly it seemed that visitors were not welcome. Another moment, and the past must be forgotten—the present rejoined.

*A rising moon, enlarged by the camera's telephoto lens, backlights
the chimneys of the Bi-Metalic Mill.*

BIBLIOGRAPHY

Bartlett, Richard A. *Great Surveys of the American West*, The American Exploration and Travel Series, vol. 39. Norman, Okla.: University of Oklahoma Press, 1962.

Beebe, Lucius M., and Clegg, C. M. *The American West: The Pictorial Epic of a Continent.* New York: E. P. Dutton & Co., Inc., 1955.

Carey, Charles H. *A General History of Oregon Prior to 1861.* 2 vols. Portland, Ore.: Metropolitan Press, 1935-36.

Chatterton, Governor. *Yesterday's Wyoming.* Aurora, Colo., 1957.

Coutant, Charles G. *The History of Wyoming from the Earliest Known Discoveries.* 2 vols. Laramie, Wyo.: Chaplin, Spafford & Mathison, 1899.

Crossroads of the West; Fremont County, Wyoming, Jubilee Book. Lander, Wyo., 1968.

Dimsdale, Thomas J. *The Vigilantes of Montana.* Norman, Okla.: University of Oklahoma Press, 1953.

Donaldson, Thomas C. *Idaho of Yesterday.* Introduction by Thomas B. Donaldson. Caldwell, Idaho: The Caxton Printers, Ltd., 1941.

Driggs, Howard R. *Westward America.* With reproductions of 40 water color paintings by William H. Jackson. Trails Edition. New York: G. P. Putnam's Sons, 1942.

Erwin, Marie H. *Wyoming Historical Blue Book.* 1946.

Fisher, Vardis, and Holmes, Opal Laurel. *Gold Rushes and Mining Camps of the Early American West.* Caldwell, Idaho: The Caxton Printers, Ltd., 1968.

Florin, Lambert. *Ghost Town Album.* Seattle, Wash.: Superior Publishing Company, 1962.

————. *Western Ghost Towns.* Seattle, Wash.: Superior Publishing Company, 1961

Grant's Pass (Ore.) *Daily Courier*, 3 April 1935; 2 April 1960.

Hafen, LeRoy R. *The Overland Mail, 1849-1869; Promoter of Settlement, Precursor of Railroads.* Cleveland, Ohio: The Arthur H. Clark Company, 1926.

Hamilton, James McLellan. *From Wilderness to Statehood; A History of Montana, 1805-1900.* Foreword by A. L. Strand; edited by Merrill G. Burlingame. 3 vols. Portland, Ore.; Binfords & Mort, 1957.

Hebard, Grace Raymond, and Brininstool, E. A. *The Bozeman Trail; Historical Accounts of the Blazing of the Overland Routes into the*

Northwest, and the Fights with Red Cloud's Warriors. 2 vols. Cleveland, Ohio: The Arthur H. Clark Company, 1922.

Heritage, vol. 2, no. 1 (December, 1963). A publication of the Okanogan County (Wash.) Historical Society.

Howard, Joseph Kinsey. *Montana; High, Wide, and Handsome.* New Haven, Conn.: Yale University Press, 1943.

————. *Montana Margins, A State Anthology.* New Haven, Conn.: Yale University Press, 1946.

Idaho, Federal Writers' Projects. *Idaho: A Guide in Word and Picture.* American Guide Series. Caldwell, Idaho: The Caxton Printers, Ltd., 1937.

Idaho Yesterdays, vol. 9, no. 1 (Boise, Idaho, 1965). A publication of the Idaho Historical Society.

Jackson, Joseph Henry. *Gold Rush Album.* New York: Charles Scribner's Sons, 1949.

Jackson, William Henry. *Picture Maker of the Old West*, with text based on diaries and notebooks, ed. by Clarence S. Jackson. New York: Charles Scribner's Sons, 1947.

Miller, Nina H. *Shutters West.* Denver: Sage Books, 1962.

Mining Catalog for the Mining Industry (for metal and nonmetallic open pit). New York, 1949.

Mining in Idaho, Ref. No. 9 (Boise, Idaho, n.d.). A publication of the Idaho Historical Society.

Montana, Federal Writers' Project. *Montana: A State Guide Book.* American Guide Series. New York: Hastings House [c1939].

Nevins, Allan. *Fremont, Pathmarker of the West.* New ed. New York: Longmans, Green & Co., Inc., 1955.

Okanogan (Wash.) *Independent*, numerous issues.

Oregon, Workers of the Writers' Program. *Oregon: End of the Trail.* American Guide Series. Portland, Ore.: Binfords & Mort, Publishers [c1940].

Pence, Mary Lou, and Homsher, Lola M. The *Ghost Towns of Wyoming.* New York: Hastings House. 1957.

Portland (Ore.) *Oregonian*, 7 September 1943; 9 September 1943.

Ramsey, Guy Reed. *Postmarked Washington.* N.d. A publication of the Okanogan County (Wash.) Historical Society.

Rickey, Don, Jr. *Forty Miles a Day on Beans and Hay; The Enlisted Soldier Fighting the Indian Wars.* Norman, Okla.: University of Oklahoma Press, 1963.

Salem (Ore.) *Capitol Journal*, 26 August 1964.

Sollid, Roberta Beed. *Calamity Jane: A Study in Historical Criticism.* Correlated and edited by Vivian A. Paladin. Helena, Mont.: Historical Society of Montana, 1958.

Stewart, W. E., and associates. *Idaho's Bonanza Years.* Hailey, Idaho, 1966.

United States Forest Service. Maps of the National Forests of the Northwestern States.

United States Geological Survey. *Bulletins*, 364, 580C, 580G, 626, 804, 811D.

————. *Professional Paper* No. 25.

————. Topographic maps of all areas known to carry mineralization in the Northwestern States.

Washington, Writers' Program. *Washington: A Guide to the Evergreen State*. American Guide Series. Portland, Ore.: Binfords & Mort, Publishers, 1941.

Webb, Todd. *Gold Strikes and Ghost Towns*. New York: Doubleday & Company, Inc, 1961.

Wolle, Muriel Sibell *Montana Pay Dirt: A Guide to the Mining Camps of the Treasure State*. Denver: Sage Books, 1963.

————. *The Bonanza Trail: Ghost Towns and Mining Camps of the West*. Bloomington, Ind.: Indiana University Press, 1953.

Wyoming, Writers' Program. *Wyoming: A Guide to Its History, Highways, and People American Guide Series*. New York: Oxford University Press, 1941.

INDEX